THE POWER OF POSITIVE ATTITUDE

A Roadmap to Success

MS. RESHMI MENON | DR. RAJAT PATHAK

INDIA • SINGAPORE • MALAYSIA

Table of Contents

Introduction

Success is a destination that many aspire to reach, yet the paths we take to get there can be vastly different. While talent, skill, and effort play fundamental roles in achieving our goals, there is one often-overlooked factor that can make a world of difference, and that is "**Attitude.**" In this book, we will explore the great impact of a positive attitude on the journey to success. .

A positive attitude isn't just about putting on a smile or maintaining a shallow sense of optimism. It's a mindset – a way of thinking and approaching life's challenges with resilience, confidence, and hope. It's about understanding that setbacks are opportunities in disguise and that our beliefs and thoughts shape our reality.

Throughout the chapters that follow, we will probe and investigate the science behind positivity, the transformative power of mindset, the importance of resilience, and the role of optimism in achieving your dreams. You'll discover how self-confidence, positive relationships, goal-setting, and persistence are all interconnected with maintaining a positive attitude.

We will also explore the significance of adaptability, mindfulness, and emotional intelligence in your pursuit for success, as well as the role of gratitude and a positive work environment in nurturing your growth. You'll learn to overcome the inherent negativity bias that often clouds our judgement and discover how celebrating your achievements can reinforce your positive habits.

Ultimately, this book is a roadmap – a guide to help you navigate the sometimes challenging terrain of life and reach your destination of success. It's not a guarantee of an easy journey, but it is a promise that a positive attitude can be your most powerful friend along the way.

So, are you ready to embark on this transformative journey towards a more positive, successful, and fulfilling life? If your answer is "Yes," then let's begin.

Preface

In our short lives, we come across many people. Some individuals instantly appeal to us in the first meeting, even though we may not know them well, yet something magnetic about their positive energy pulls us towards them. It's like a magnetic person drawing us in, even without direct interaction. On the other hand, there are those whom we don't find likeable right from the initial encounter, even though they haven't behaved poorly towards us. Have you ever wondered why this happens?

Well, my father used to always make a statement – "Every person emits a certain energy. We refer to this energy as "aura." Whether this energy is positive or negative determines our liking or disliking towards that person. It goes beyond their actions; it's about the underlying energy that influences our perception of the individual." This statement of his made a lot of sense to me in the later years of my life when I started dealing with people; and I understood that this phenomenon suggests that there is an intangible quality within each person that affects our feelings about them. This quality, or "aura," can be either positive or negative, influencing our initial impressions. Even before we get to know someone well, this energy shapes our perception of them. The level of positivity or negativity in this energy determines whether we are drawn to or repelled by that person. Essentially, our first impressions are not solely based on observable behaviour but are also influenced by this subtle energy that each person carries.

This "aura" is nothing but a reflection of our own personality, which we nowadays refer to as "attitude," "personality," or "character."

In this book, we will analyse the numerous benefits of maintaining a positive mindset, thereby shedding light on why such a mental attitude is essential and how it impacts our lives. We will delve into how positive thinking can enhance our lives and influence our personalities.

Firstly, keeping a positive mindset ensures that our thoughts and emotions remain pure and constructive. This helps us in facing challenges and adversities, maintaining a prosperous and balanced perspective. Positive thinking brings inner peace and composure, leading to happiness and prosperity in our lives.

Maintaining a positive outlook can also improve our relationships. It has a positive impact on our personalities, enabling us to cultivate positive connections with our family and friends. Additionally, positive thinking can contribute to the improvement of our professional lives.

It pushes us towards our goals swiftly, enabling us to overcome obstacles with flexibility.

This book will also explore why positive thinking is crucial, as it is a vital aspect of making our lives better. Positive thinking assists us in turning our dreams into reality and taps into our inner strengths. It infuses a form of mental courage that empowers us to face challenges with confidence.

Through these analyses, the book aims to help readers understand the significance of positive thinking and guide them in reaping its benefits in their lives.

To our guiding stars, our respective Fathers

– 1 –

Defining Positive Attitude

What is Positive Attitude?

In our country, there has been a longstanding proverb that goes like this - *"Dheeraj, dharm, mitra, aur nari aaptti, kaal parikhiye chaari."*

The phrase "Dheeraj, dharm, mitra, aur nari; aaptti kaal parikhiye chaari" is in Hindi and can be translated to "Patience, righteousness, friendship, and woman; examine these four during times of adversity." This phrase encapsulates important virtues and values, highlighting their significance during challenging circumstances. Let's delve into the components of the phrase:

1. **Dheeraj (Patience):** Patience is the ability to survive in difficult situations without losing composure. It suggests the importance of remaining calm and collected during times of adversity, avoiding impulsive reactions, and navigating challenges with a steady and composed mindset.

2. **Dharm (Righteousness):** Dharm refers to righteous or moral conduct. It emphasises the importance of adhering to ethical principles

and fulfilling one's duties and responsibilities. During difficult times, maintaining a sense of righteousness guides individuals to make decisions that align with moral values.

3. **Mitra (Friendship):** Friendship is highlighted as a valuable aspect during adversity. It stresses the significance of having supportive and trustworthy friends who can offer assistance, encouragement, and companionship during challenging situations. Strong friendships can provide emotional and moral support.

4. **Nari (Woman):** Nari translates to "women" in Hindi. In this context, it signifies the importance of considering and respecting the perspectives, experiences, and contributions of women during times of adversity. It underscores the need for gender equality, empathy, and support for women's rights and well-being.

5. **Aaptti Kaal (Times of Adversity):** The phrase specifically refers to "aaptti kaal" or times of adversity. This indicates that the qualities of patience, righteousness, friendship, and consideration for women are particularly relevant and crucial during difficult and trying circumstances. It suggests that one's character and values are truly tested in challenging situations.

Overall, the phrase "*Dheeraj, dharm, mitra aur nari; aaptti kaal parikhiye chaari*" urges individuals to reflect on and uphold the virtues of patience, righteousness, friendship, and consideration for women during times of adversity. It emphasises the importance of maintaining integrity, developing supportive relationships, and recognising the value of gender equality and empathy in facing challenges and overcoming obstacles.

A positive attitude, therefore, is like a lighthouse that guides us through the difficulties of life. It is a mindset characterised by optimism, resilience, and a proactive approach to challenges. Having a positive attitude means viewing the world with a hopeful and constructive outlook, even when faced with adversity.

But what exactly is a positive attitude, and how does it affect our lives and our pursuit of success?

See, a positive attitude is a mental and emotional characteristic that influences the way we interpret and respond to life's events.

Positive attitude involves "Optimism," which is the core. It is a belief that, regardless of the current circumstances, the future holds promise and opportunities for growth. Positive individuals tend to see setbacks as temporary and specific, while attributing success to their efforts and abilities.

When we talk about positivity in someone's character, you will always see that somewhere down the line, this person has bounced back from adversity, which has kept him going.

Always remember that people with a positive attitude are more resilient because they view challenges as opportunities for personal development. They adapt to change, learn from failures and persevere in the face of setbacks.

I have also closely observed that individuals with a positive attitude take proactive steps to improve their situations. They don't passively accept their circumstances, but actively seek solutions and opportunities for growth. This proactive approach empowers them to shape their lives positively.

More than being proactive, I have seen that positive souls are God-fearing individuals and are full of gratitude for what the Almighty has ushered upon them. Gratitude is an essential component of a positive attitude. It involves recognising and appreciating the positive aspects of life, even in challenging times. Gratitude promotes a sense of contentment and satisfaction.

Further, compassion also plays a role in a positive attitude. Individuals who have a positive frame of mind tend to be compassionate, understanding the feelings and perspectives of others. This compassion strengthens relationships and builds a supportive network.

The Impact of Attitude on Success

The link between attitude and success is undeniable. Your attitude shapes your actions, decisions, and the energy you bring to your pursuits.

Success in life is a multifaceted pursuit, encompassing various dimensions such as personal growth, career accomplishments, meaningful relationships, and overall fulfilment. The accomplishment of success, regardless of the specific aspect of life it pertains to, is greatly influenced by an individual's attitude. In this chapter, we will delve into the dynamic relationship between a positive attitude and success, exploring the profound impact that maintaining a positive mindset can have in unlocking your potential and achieving the success you desire.

A positive attitude is more than just a transitory emotion or a passing mood; it is a fundamental aspect of one's mindset. At its core, a positive attitude is marked by optimism, resilience, and a belief in one's capabilities. It's a firm outlook that acknowledges the possibility of success and growth in the face of challenges. A positive attitude doesn't ignore problems but views them as opportunities for learning and improvement.

One of the most visible ways in which a positive attitude influences success is through **motivation**.

A positive attitude serves as a powerful source of motivation, fuelling the drive to set and achieve goals. The optimism and enthusiasm that offshoots from a positive mindset provide the energy and determination needed to tackle challenges and persistently work towards success. It's the oil/fuel that keeps you going, even when the path seems steep and daunting.

Illustrative Example: Consider an individual starting a fitness journey. A positive attitude empowers them with the belief that they can achieve their fitness goals. This attitude keeps them motivated to maintain a consistent workout routine, make healthier dietary choices, and overcome the inevitable setbacks along the way.

Let me cite one more example, and I am sure this must have happened with most of us during our elementary school days, where we got criticised by our friends or teachers when we gave our opinion on a topic, and we felt humiliated in front of the whole class. Later, when we were tempted to offer our opinion in school or in a group of people, we held back and kept quiet... because all the while we were remembering how painful it was that day when we got criticised.

Now, just imagine if we continue to stick with this thought or event for the rest of our life, will we be able to overcome this fear of expressing ourselves ever?

I bet we will never be able to overcome this.

Whereas, on the other hand, if we sit back and think rationally… that "it was your childhood"… and now, with age and experience, we are more mature and worldly wise. Today, we can consciously choose to view the situation differently – the teacher or our friends may have disagreed with us then, but it wasn't a statement about our intelligence or our overall worth as a person!

That's where our positive attitude comes into the picture.

Always remember, it is we who must overcome our past failures. That's why they say, *"don't cry over spilt milk," look ahead, and walk again."*

There is again a saying in Hindi, *"beeti taahi bisaariye, aur aagey ki sudh le,"* which can be translated to "Learn from the past, forget about it, and focus on what lies ahead." This concept encourages individuals to reflect on their past experiences, derive lessons from them, but not dwell excessively on past mistakes or successes. Instead, it emphasises the importance of moving forward with a positive and forward-looking mindset.

The statement encourages a balanced approach to dealing with the past. It acknowledges the significance of learning from past experiences but emphasises the need to move forward with a positive and proactive mindset. By applying the lessons learned, individuals can navigate the future more effectively, free from unnecessary burdens or preoccupations with past mistakes. This concept aligns with the idea of resilience, growth, and the continuous pursuit of personal and professional development.

Resilience in the Face of Adversity

Success rarely comes without its share of setbacks and failures. However, a positive attitude equips individuals with the resilience to bounce back stronger after facing challenges. Instead of being disheartened by failures, those with a positive attitude see them as opportunities for personal growth. They view setbacks as stepping stones rather than stumbling blocks and understand that learning from mistakes is an integral part of success.

Illustrative Example: Imagine a budding entrepreneur who faces financial setbacks early in their business venture. A positive attitude encourages them to view these setbacks as valuable learning experiences. This mindset empowers them to adapt their business strategy, seek alternative sources of funding, and, eventually, succeed.

Impact on Decision-Making

Your attitude significantly influences the decisions you make in life. A positive attitude encourages more constructive and optimistic decision-making. It leads individuals to make choices that are aligned with their goals, preferences, and a broader view of success.

It empowers them to take calculated risks, seize opportunities, and contribute to their success.

Illustrative Example: A person with a positive attitude, who is contemplating a career change, will approach the decision with optimism. They will be more likely to weigh the potential benefits of the change and the alignment with their long-term goals. This mindset could lead to a decision to pursue a career that ultimately brings them greater satisfaction and success.

> *Virtually nothing on earth can stop a person............ With a positive attitude who has his goal clarity in sight*
>
> **Denis Waitley**

Leadership and Teamwork

Positive attitudes are often associated with effective leadership. Leaders with a positive attitude can inspire and motivate their teams to achieve success. Their optimism and encouragement create a positive work environment, enhancing employee morale, teamwork, and, in turn, the overall success of the organisation.

Illustrative Example: Think of a manager who leads a team with a positive attitude. They encourage open communication, acknowledge achievements, and provide constructive feedback. This leadership style fosters a work environment in which employees are motivated, collaborate effectively, and contribute to the organisation's success.

Problem-Solving and Creativity

A positive attitude can spark creative problem-solving and innovation. Those with a positive mindset view challenges as opportunities for growth and creativity. They are more likely to think outside the box, explore new solutions, and find innovative approaches to overcome obstacles.

Illustrative Example: An inventor facing technical difficulties in developing a new product is empowered by a positive attitude. They view these challenges as opportunities to enhance their invention, rather than insurmountable hurdles. This mindset encourages them to brainstorm innovative solutions, adapt their design, and eventually bring a groundbreaking product to the market.

Building Meaningful Relationships

Success often depends on building strong relationships and networks. A positive attitude can be a magnet for attracting valuable connections. Individuals who approach interactions with a positive attitude establish meaningful professional relationships that can lead to career opportunities, collaborations, and mentorship.

Illustrative Example: Consider someone attending a networking event with a positive attitude. They approach others with a friendly and open mindset, leading to engaging conversations and the establishment of meaningful connections. These connections can later lead to career opportunities, collaborative projects, and professional growth.

Health and Well-Being

A positive attitude extends to one's physical and mental well-being. It can lead to a healthier lifestyle, better stress management, and overall well-being. Those with a positive attitude tend to take better care of their health, providing them with the energy and resilience required to pursue their goals and achieve success.

Illustrative Example: An individual facing a health challenge can benefit greatly from a positive attitude. This mindset enables them to maintain hope and determination, positively affecting their treatment outcomes. The emotional resilience stemming from a positive attitude can also reduce stress, improve mental health and enhance the overall quality of life.

Adaptability in a Changing World

Success in a rapidly changing world often necessitates adaptability. A positive attitude fosters open-mindedness and a willingness to embrace change. Those with a positive attitude view changes, whether in technology, markets, or personal circumstances, as opportunities for growth. They invest in learning new skills and adapting to emerging trends, positioning themselves for long-term success.

Illustrative Example: Imagine a professional in a technology-related field with a positive attitude. They view technological advancements as opportunities for growth rather than threats to their current skill set. This mindset encourages them to continuously acquire new knowledge, adapt to changing industry trends, and remain relevant and successful.

Conclusion

Unlocking Potential and Achieving Success with a Positive Attitude,

In this chapter, we have explored the profound impact of maintaining a positive attitude on unlocking one's potential and achieving success. A positive attitude is not just a passive reflection of success; it is an active catalyst that propels individuals toward their goals and aspirations. It shapes motivation, resilience, decision-making, leadership, creativity, relationships, well-being, and adaptability. Success is not merely the result of external factors; it is deeply rooted in one's attitude and outlook. By nurturing a positive attitude, one can harness its remarkable power to unlock their potential and pave the way to the success they desire in various aspects of life. A positive attitude is a powerful tool that transforms obstacles into opportunities and makes the pursuit of success an attainable and fulfilling journey.

− 2 −
The Mindset Shift

The concept of mindset has gained significant attention in recent years, with researchers and self-help enthusiasts emphasising its deep impact on personal development and success. This chapter explores the idea of a mindset shift, the process of changing one's mindset from a fixed to a growth orientation. We probe into the importance of recognising negative thought patterns that hinder growth and discuss strategies to cultivate a growth mindset. By understanding and implementing these principles, individuals can enhance their ability to learn, adapt, and succeed in various aspects of life.

Introduction

Mindset refers to a person's inherent beliefs and attitudes that shape their perception of themselves and the world around them. Two primary mindsets have been extensively studied: **the fixed mindset** and **the growth mindset**.

A fixed mindset is characterised by the belief that abilities and intelligence are static traits, while a growth mindset asserts that these qualities can be developed through effort, learning and perseverance.

This chapter explores the process of changing one's mindset, the recognition of negative thought patterns associated with a fixed mindset, and strategies for cultivating a growth mindset.

Changing Your Mindset

Always remember one thing in life, if you want to move forward, then you will have to bring about a change in your thinking and in your mindset.

Imagine you have a goal, like learning to play a musical instrument. Initially, you might think it will only take five steps to become proficient. These steps could include buying the instrument, finding a teacher, practicing regularly, mastering basic tunes, and, finally, playing more complex compositions.

However, as you delve into the learning process, you realise there's more to it. You may need to learn about music theory, explore different genres, attend concerts, and practice with dedication. Instead of just five steps, you find there are 155 steps involved in becoming a truly skilled musician.

But, when you are committed and are willing to do whatever it takes, you begin to attract the people and circumstances necessary to accomplish your goals.

As you embark on this musical journey, your commitment starts to influence your surroundings. You become part of a community of musicians, attracting like-minded people who share your passion. Maybe you join a band, attend workshops, or collaborate with others. Your commitment not only helps you personally but also draws in the circumstances and people necessary for your musical aspirations.

In everyday life, this commitment and willingness to take steps, whether few or many, can be applied to various scenarios. Let's say you aspire to start a small business. Initially, you may think it requires just a few key steps, like creating a business plan, securing funding, and launching your product or service.

However, as you delve deeper, you realise there are numerous intricacies involved, such as marketing strategies, customer engagement, and adapting to market trends. Regardless of the complexity, your commitment drives you to take every step needed for success. This commitment not only propels you forward but also attracts potential clients, collaborators, and opportunities that align with your business goals.

In essence, the concept "changing your mindset" is about recognising that goals often involve more steps than initially anticipated. Yet, by making a firm commitment and being willing to take all the necessary steps, you not only progress towards your goal but also create an environment that attracts the support and circumstances needed for your success. It's a powerful reminder that dedication and persistence can significantly influence the journey towards achieving your aspirations.

The concept we are describing here is often referred to as determination, perseverance, or a dedicated mental attitude. It reflects a mindset of unwavering commitment and persistence towards achieving one's goals, regardless of the challenges or obstacles that may arise along the way.

Here's a breakdown of the key elements of this mental attitude:

1. **Self-awareness**

   The first step in changing your mindset is self-awareness. It involves acknowledging your current mindset and understanding how it may be limiting your potential. Self-awareness can be facilitated through introspection, journaling, or seeking feedback from others. It's essential to recognise that everyone possesses a mix of fixed and growth mindsets in different areas of life, and it's possible to shift one's mindset over time.

2. **Adopt the growth mindset**

   To transition from a fixed mindset to a growth mindset, one must fully adopt the concept that abilities can be developed. This shift in belief is fundamental to the process. It involves challenging and changing deeply inherent beliefs about your abilities and potential. Reading books, articles, or listening to talks on the subject of growth mindset can help reinforce this shift in perspective.

3. **Challenge your comfort zone**

    Stepping out of your comfort zone is crucial for developing a growth mindset. Accept challenges and view failures as opportunities for growth. When you encounter difficulties, remind yourself that setbacks are part of the learning process. Seek challenges that push your boundaries and provide opportunities to acquire new skills.

EXAMPLE: Leander Paes

Leander Paes, the legendary Indian tennis player, faced early setbacks and struggled to find success before transforming his career. Here's a unique real story of his journey:

Early Career:

–   1989-1993: Leander Paes was a young and promising tennis player, but his mindset and limited efforts were limiting his potential. He played on the junior circuit and participated in a few low-profile tournaments, but major success eluded him.

Turning Point

Leander Paes reached a pivotal moment in his career, realising that he needed to break free from his self-imposed limitations. He sought feedback from his coach and mentors who encouraged him to challenge himself, work harder, and step out of his comfort zone.

Transformation:

- 1994: Paes revamped his training regimen, focusing on improving his physical fitness and mental resilience.
- 1995: He decided to compete on the international circuit, setting his sights on tournaments around the world.

Rising Through the Ranks:

- 1996: Paes made a significant breakthrough by reaching the semi-finals of the men's singles event at the Atlanta Olympics. Although he didn't win a medal, it was a remarkable achievement for an Indian tennis player.

World Stage Success:

- 1999: Paes partnered with Mahesh Bhupathi in doubles, and their partnership quickly gained recognition. They reached the finals of the Wimbledon Championships.

- 2001: Paes and Bhupathi clinched the French Open men's doubles title, marking their first Grand Slam victory.
- 2003: They secured the Australian Open men's doubles title.

Olympic Glory and More Titles:

- 2004: Leander Paes, along with his partner Mahesh Bhupathi, won a historic tennis medal for India at the Athens Olympics, earning a bronze in the men's doubles.
- 2006: Paes achieved the career Grand Slam in mixed doubles and men's doubles.
- 2010-2011: He continued to add to his impressive list of grand slam titles, capturing the Australian Open and the US Open, with different partners.
- 2016: Leander Paes, at the age of 43, participated in the Rio Olympics. He didn't secure a medal, but displayed remarkable commitment and sportsmanship.

Legacy

Leander Paes' story is one of tremendous personal growth, persistence, and the ability to turn failures into stepping stones towards success. He didn't let early limitations define him; instead, he used them as fuel to push his boundaries and acquire new skills. His journey from early struggles to being a consistent contender on the world tennis stage, earning medals at the Olympics, and winning multiple Grand Slam titles, serves as an inspiration to aspiring Indian tennis players.

Leander Paes' remarkable career has left an indelible mark on Indian tennis and continues to inspire generations of athletes to aim high, work hard, and never be deterred by initial setbacks.

Recognising Negative Thought Patterns

1. Fixed mindset triggers - To recognise negative thought patterns associated with a fixed mindset, it's important to identify common triggers:

- Avoidance of challenges: Individuals with a fixed mindset tend to avoid challenges to protect their self-esteem. They fear failure and may opt for easier tasks to maintain a sense of competence.
- Negative self-talk: Fixed mindset individuals often engage in negative self-talk, telling themselves they're not good enough or intelligent enough to succeed.
- Comparisons: Constantly comparing oneself to others can reinforce a fixed mindset, as it often leads to feelings of inadequacy or superiority.
- Defensiveness: Fixed mindset individuals become defensive in the face of criticism or feedback, as they perceive it as a personal attack, rather than an opportunity for growth.

2. Self-reflection: To combat these triggers, engage in self-reflection. Whenever you notice yourself avoiding challenges, engaging in negative self-talk, making unhealthy comparisons, or becoming defensive, pause and ask yourself...

Why???

Ask yourself this question... and give yourself a correct answer.

Trust, no one knows you better than you yourself...

Try to understand the underlying fixed mindset belief that's driving these reactions.

3. Replace negative thoughts: Once you've identified negative thought patterns, work on replacing them with growth-oriented beliefs.

Instead of saying, "I can't do this," shift your mindset to "I can't do this yet." By adding "yet," you acknowledge the potential for growth and improvement.

EXAMPLE

Entrepreneurs often grapple with self-doubt and uncertainty. Recognising and addressing these negative thought patterns is vital for embracing the new mindset of entrepreneurship in India.

Real-Life Example 1: Ritesh Agarwal, Founder of OYO.

Early Career and Self-Doubt:

- 2012: Ritesh Agarwal, a young entrepreneur from India, embarked on a journey to transform the hospitality industry. He founded OYO, envisioning a network of budget hotels. However, like many entrepreneurs, he grappled with self-doubt and uncertainty.

Challenges and Setbacks:

- 2013-2014: OYO initially struggled to gain traction. Ritesh faced challenges in scaling the business, and he often questioned whether he was on the right path. Rejections and scepticism from potential investors and partners added to his doubts.

Turning Point

Instead of succumbing to self-doubt, Ritesh Agarwal recognised these negative thought patterns as opportunities for growth and innovation.

Innovative Pivot:

- 2015: Ritesh analysed feedback and market trends. He realised that the key to success was not just affordable accommodation but also a consistent and high-quality guest experience. OYO pivoted to a franchise model, partnering with small hotel owners and ensuring a standardised experience for guests.

Rapid Growth:

- 2016-2017: OYO's new model quickly gained momentum. The innovative approach addressed the concerns of both customers and partners, leading to rapid expansion.

Revenue Growth:

- 2018: OYO's revenue saw substantial growth, reaching a significant milestone as a unicorn startup in the hospitality sector. The unique franchise model and technology-driven solutions set them apart.

Global Expansion:

- 2019-2020: OYO expanded its footprint internationally, becoming a recognised name in several countries, including the United States, China, and Europe.

Success in the Hospitality Industry

Today, OYO is one of the world's largest and most successful hospitality brands, offering a wide range of accommodations from budget to luxury. Ritesh Agarwal's ability to recognise and address self-doubt, learn from rejections, and pivot the business model has not only made him a successful entrepreneur but has also disrupted the hospitality industry.

Ritesh's journey from uncertainty to success serves as a testament to the power of resilience and the ability to transform negative thought patterns into motivation and innovation. His story continues to inspire aspiring entrepreneurs worldwide, demonstrating that, with determination and adaptability, it's possible to achieve success, even when faced with initial setbacks and doubts.

Cultivating a Growth Mindset

We all must have heard this statement from our elders during our childhood that there are two types of people in the world – one with a positive thinking and the other with a negative set of mind. And now to find out who is positive and who is negative, just give them a glass of water half filled. Now the one with a positive mindset will say, "the glass is half full," and the negative thinker will say, "the glass is half empty."

We all see the world through our lenses, which we can refer to as filters as well. These filters are our own perceptions. Let me explain further…

Every person sees only what he wants to see according to his choice... or we can also say that _he sees only what he thinks_.

If he thinks good and positive about the world and people, then he will see happiness, joy, prosperity around him. Having said that, if he has a pessimistic or negative approach to life, then he will see gloomy, morose, and sorrowful faces around him. Now it is your decision as to which lens you want to see the world through.

Let me further elaborate... remember when we were young... or just observe a little child... his consciousness, his attitude, and approach towards everything around him are POSITIVE and UPBEAT. When he stumbles and falls, what does he do? I will tell you what he doesn't do. He doesn't frown or blame the floor and ground, he doesn't point fingers at his parents for giving him lousy instructions, and most importantly, he doesn't quit. What he does is... he smiles, gets up again, makes another attempt, and another, and another until he succeeds...

I am sure you got the gist of the above...

His lenses are spick and span, and he feels that he can conquer the world.

But this same child, when growing older, starts complaining, criticising people, and ridiculing peers for his uncertain life situations. The dust of complaint, criticism, starts depositing on his lenses, and his vision towards life becomes blurred. He gives up his dreams – all because he failed to clean his lenses.

Rather, if this child had changed his attitude, the whole new world would have opened up for him.

Do you see what I meant when I say that we all see the world through our lenses? Can you appreciate how your positive attitude affects the way you see everything in your life? More importantly, you are beginning to see those areas where your lens needs to be washed?

It's your job to keep your lenses clean. Sure, there will be people out there to encourage you, but in the end, nobody else can do it for you. This is called a GROWTH MINDSET.

A growth mindset is the belief that abilities and intelligence can be developed through dedication and hard work. It is crucial for entrepreneurs to cultivate this mindset to navigate the challenges of the business world,

1. Adapt learning and effort

In a growth mindset, learning and effort are seen as opportunities for development rather than burdens. Embrace challenges and setbacks as chances to learn and grow. Understand that mastery in any field requires continuous effort and practice.

2. Set meaningful goals

Setting meaningful, achievable goals is essential for cultivating a growth mindset. These goals provide direction and motivation. Break them down into smaller, manageable steps and celebrate your progress along the way. This approach reinforces the belief that effort leads to improvement.

3. Seek feedback and learn from failures

Feedback, even if it's critical, is invaluable for growth. Take feedback as a tool for improvement, not as a threat to your self-worth. Similarly, view failures as opportunities to learn and refine your approach. Understand that setbacks are a natural part of the journey towards mastery.

4. Surround yourself with growth-oriented individuals

Surrounding yourself with people who possess a growth mindset can be highly influential. Their attitudes and behaviours can inspire and support your own growth-oriented mindset. Engage in discussions with such individuals and learn from their experiences.

Real-Life Example 2: Byju Raveendran, Founder of BYJU'S.

2011 – The Birth of BYJU'S

In 2011, Byju Raveendran, an engineer and passionate educator from India, founded BYJU'S. His vision was clear: to transform the education landscape in India through digital learning. At a time when traditional classroom teaching dominated the education sector, Byju recognised the need for innovative and engaging learning solutions.

Early Struggles and Continuous Learning:

- 2011-2014: In the initial years, BYJU'S faced significant challenges. The concept of digital learning was relatively new in India, and it wasn't an easy path. Byju, however, had a growth mindset. He was open to feedback and actively sought insights from students and teachers to understand their needs better. This approach allowed him to continuously adapt and improve the content.

Expanding Offerings:

- 2014-2016: As BYJU'S refined its digital learning content, it expanded its offerings to cater to students across various educational levels, including school students preparing for exams, and competitive exams like JEE and NEET. The company's comprehensive approach attracted a wider user base.

Exponential Growth and Revenue Model:

- 2017-2018: *BYJU'S witnessed exponential growth as it not only provided video lessons but also introduced interactive quizzes, personalised learning paths, and in-depth analytics to track student progress. This innovative approach not only helped students learn, but also provided valuable insights to parents and teachers. The freemium model, where basic content was available for free, and premium features were offered through subscriptions, became a significant part of their revenue model.

Global Expansion and Strategic Partnerships:

- 2019-2020: BYJU'S expanded its reach globally, reaching students outside of India's borders. The company secured strategic partnerships with educational institutions, both in India and abroad, to further enhance its content offerings and attract more users. This expansion and collaboration played a pivotal role in increasing revenue.

Pandemic Acceleration:

- 2020-2021: The COVID-19 pandemic accelerated the adoption of online learning. With schools and coaching centres closed, students and parents turned to digital education platforms. BYJU'S saw a substantial increase in revenue during this time as it quickly adapted to cater to the surge in demand.

Success in Ed-Tech

Today, BYJU'S is one of the world's leading ed-tech companies. Byju Raveendran's visionary approach, willingness to embrace change, and dedication to improving educational outcomes have made BYJU'S a global success in the ed-tech industry. The company continues to expand its offerings, making quality education accessible to millions of students.

Byju Raveendran's journey is a testament to the transformative power of continuous learning and adaptation. It exemplifies the impact of combining innovation, technology, and a growth mindset to address the evolving needs of the education sector. His story serves as an inspiration to entrepreneurs and educators worldwide.

Real-Life Example 3: Paytm and Vijay Shekhar Sharma

2010 - The Birth of Paytm:

In 2010, Vijay Shekhar Sharma, a visionary entrepreneur from India, founded Paytm, a digital payment company. He recognised the untapped potential of digital payments in a country where cash transactions were the norm.

Facing Established Competition:

–   2010-2012: Paytm entered an industry already dominated by established players. Digital payments were not widely adopted in India at the time, and the competition was fierce. Despite these challenges, Sharma persisted, believing in the transformative potential of digital payments in the country.

Continuous Improvement and Adaptation:

–   2013-2014: Paytm focused on continuous improvement, enhancing user experience, and expanding the services it offered. The platform evolved from being primarily a mobile recharge service to a comprehensive digital wallet, allowing users to pay for a wide range of products and services.

Growth Mindset and Financial Services:

- 2015-2016: Vijay Shekhar Sharma exemplified a growth mindset by identifying opportunities beyond just payments. Paytm diversified its services, launching Paytm Mall (an e-commerce platform) and Paytm Payments Bank, which provided a range of financial services, including savings accounts, fixed deposits, and insurance. This strategic diversification led to increased revenue streams and customer engagement.

Demonetisation Boost:

- Late 2016: India's demonetisation policy, which aimed to reduce the use of physical cash, proved to be a turning point. Paytm experienced a significant surge in users as people turned to digital payment methods. The company capitalised on this opportunity and expanded further.

Explosive Growth and Revenue Model:

- 2017-2018: Paytm's user base continued to grow exponentially. Its revenue model evolved from primarily facilitating mobile recharges to encompassing a broad spectrum of services. It generated revenue through transaction fees, commissions from merchants, and the financial services it offered through Paytm Payments Bank.

IPO and Future Outlook:

- 2021: Paytm went public with its initial public offering (IPO), making it one of the biggest in India's history. The successful IPO marked a significant milestone in Paytm's journey.

Success in Digital Payments

Today, Paytm is one of India's leading digital payment and financial services companies. Vijay Shekhar Sharma's unwavering belief in the potential of digital payments, his dedication to continuous improvement, and his strategic diversification into financial services have made Paytm a prominent player in the industry.

Vijay Shekhar Sharma's story is a testament to the transformative power of embracing a growth mindset, adapting to changing market dynamics, and seizing opportunities when they arise. His journey serves as an inspiration to entrepreneurs and innovators worldwide, illustrating how persistence and vision can lead to success in highly competitive industries.

Conclusion

The mindset shift from a fixed to a growth orientation is a powerful tool for personal development and success. By recognising negative thought patterns associated with a fixed mindset and actively cultivating a growth mindset, individuals can unlock their full potential, become more resilient in the face of challenges, and achieve higher levels of proficiency and happiness in various aspects of life. Changing your mindset is not a one-time event, but an ongoing process that requires self-awareness, effort, and a commitment to growth.

The transformation of India's business landscape exemplifies a paradigm shift in mindset. The "Make in India" campaign, improved ease of doing business, and government initiatives have created a more conducive environment for entrepreneurs. Real-life examples of entrepreneurs like Ritesh Agarwal, Byju Raveendran, and Vijay Shekhar Sharma demonstrate how recognising negative thought patterns and cultivating a growth mindset can lead to entrepreneurial success.

Entrepreneurs in India and around the world can draw inspiration from these examples and the changing mindset towards business in India. By embracing new opportunities, persisting in the face of challenges, and cultivating a growth mindset, individuals can contribute to the ongoing transformation of India's business landscape and achieve their entrepreneurial aspirations.

– 3 –

Embracing Resilience

Resilience (flexibility), often defined as the ability to bounce back from adversity, has emerged as a critical factor in personal and professional success. This chapter explores the concept of resilience, its connection to achieving goals, and the strategies for building and cultivating resilience skills. Additionally, we delve into the importance of learning from setbacks as a means to enhance one's resilience and, ultimately, reach greater levels of success.

Introduction

Resilience is a comprehensive trait that involves one's ability to adapt, recover, and grow in the face of adversity, challenges, and setbacks. While success is often measured by accomplishments and achievements, it is resilience that underpins the journey towards these goals. This chapter aims to shed light on the integral role resilience plays in attaining success, the ways individuals can build and nurture resilience skills, and the significance of learning from setbacks in strengthening one's resilience.

Resilience and Success

Resilience, often described as the ability to bounce back from adversity or setbacks, is crucial in both personal and professional contexts. Let's look at a day-to-day example to illustrate the importance of resilience:

Imagine you're working on a challenging project at your job, and you encounter unexpected obstacles or setbacks. This could be anything from tight deadlines, unforeseen complications, or even interpersonal conflicts within the team. Without resilience, these challenges might be overwhelming, leading to stress, frustration, and potentially giving up on the project.

Now, consider a resilient individual in the same scenario. Despite facing setbacks, they remain adaptable and flexible. They assess the situation, learn from the challenges, and adjust their approach accordingly. They might seek support from colleagues, find alternative solutions, or even reevaluate their initial plans.

In a personal context, let's say you're working towards a personal goal, like maintaining a healthy lifestyle. You face a busy week, making it difficult to stick to your exercise routine and healthy eating habits. A person lacking resilience might see this as a failure and give up on their goal altogether. On the other hand, a resilient individual would recognise the challenges, adapt their schedule, maybe incorporate shorter workouts, or choose healthier meal options when time is limited, but still stay committed to their overall goal.

In these examples, resilience is not about avoiding challenges, but rather about facing them head-on, learning from the experience, and adapting one's approach to overcome difficulties. In the long run, individuals who develop and demonstrate resilience are better equipped to navigate the complexities of life, both in their personal and professional spheres, leading to greater success and well-being.

The Role of Resilience

Resilience is the inner strength that allows individuals to withstand adversity, bounce back from setbacks, and, ultimately, achieve success. It's not about avoiding challenges, but about developing the capacity to navigate them effectively.

1. Resilience as a Foundation

Resilience serves as the foundation upon which success is built. It provides individuals with the capacity to endure hardships, overcome obstacles, and persist in the pursuit of their goals. Success is rarely a linear journey; it is marked by trials, failures, and moments of doubt.

Resilience equips individuals with the mental and emotional fortitude to weather these storms and keep moving forward.

2. Maintaining Motivation

Resilience is closely linked to motivation and perseverance. When faced with setbacks or failures, resilient individuals are more likely to maintain their motivation and remain committed to their objectives. They view obstacles as opportunities for growth and continue to strive for their goals, even in the face of adversity.

Real-life examples vividly illustrate how resilience and success are interconnected.

Real-Life Example 1: Oprah Winfrey

Background: Oprah Winfrey, a media mogul, talk show host, and philanthropist, faced numerous hardships during her early life. She grew up in poverty, faced abuse, and had a challenging childhood.

Oprah's resilience was evident when she refused to let her troubled past define her future. She worked diligently as a radio host, then as a TV news anchor, before hosting her own talk show, "The Oprah Winfrey Show." Despite facing rejection and criticism early in her career, Oprah persevered. Her talk show became a massive success, making her one of the wealthiest and most influential women in the world.

Resilience Skills Demonstrated:

- Positive thinking: Oprah focused on her strengths and aspirations, not dwelling on her challenging past.
- Setting goals: She had a clear vision of her career goals and worked persistently to achieve them.
- Building a support system: Oprah surrounded herself with mentors and supporters who encouraged her journey.

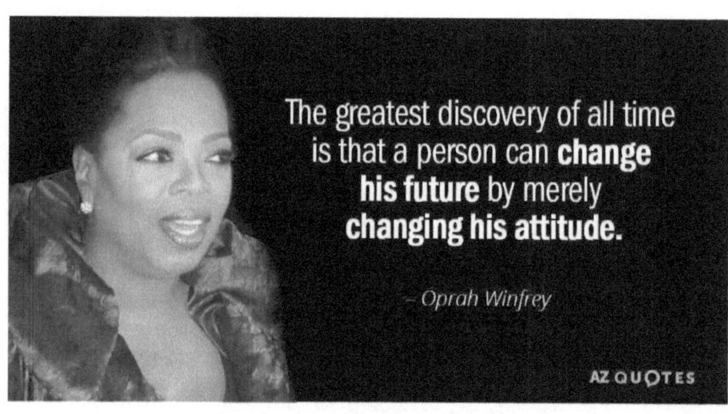

Building Resilience Skills

Developing resilience skills is an ongoing process. Let us explore some practical ways to build and strengthen resilience:

1. Developing Self-Awareness

Self-awareness is the first step in building resilience. Understanding one's strengths, weaknesses, and emotional triggers can help individuals respond more effectively to challenges. By recognising their reactions to adversity, individuals can learn to manage their emotions and make rational decisions under pressure.

2. Cultivating a Growth Mindset

A growth mindset, as discussed in previous pages, is essential for building resilience. Holding the belief that challenges and failures are opportunities for learning and growth can significantly enhance one's ability to bounce back from setbacks. It enables individuals to view setbacks as temporary, rather than undefeatable.

3. Building a Support Network

Social support is a crucial element in resilience-building. Developing a strong support network of friends, family, mentors, and colleagues can provide emotional sustenance during difficult times. These connections can offer guidance, encouragement, and a sense of belonging that strengthens resilience.

4. Practicing Stress Management

Resilience involves managing stress effectively. Implementing stress reduction techniques, such as mindfulness, meditation, or regular exercise, can help individuals maintain their composure and clarity when facing adversity.

Certain real-life examples

Real-Life Example 2: Nelson Mandela

Background: Nelson Mandela, South Africa's first Black president, spent 27 years in prison for his anti-apartheid activism. He endured harsh conditions, but he emerged from prison with an unbroken spirit.

Building Resilience Skills:

- *Positive Thinking*: While in prison, Mandela maintained a positive outlook and never wavered in his commitment to justice and equality.
- *Adaptability:* After his release, Mandela transitioned from prisoner to president, guiding

South Africa through a peaceful transition from apartheid to democracy.

- **Learning from Setbacks**: Mandela forgave his oppressors and sought reconciliation, rather than revenge, demonstrating the ability to learn from adversity.

Real-Life Example 3: J.K. Rowling

Background: Before becoming a renowned author of the Harry Potter series, J.K. Rowling faced a series of personal setbacks. She was a struggling single mother living on welfare.

Building Resilience Skills:.

- *Positive Thinking*: Despite her difficulties, Rowling never gave up on her dream of becoming a writer. She saw challenges as stepping stones.
- *Adaptability:* She adapted to her circumstances, writing in cafes while her daughter napped. She was flexible in her approach to achieving her goals.
- **Learning from Setbacks**: Rowling's manuscript was rejected by multiple publishers before finding success. Each rejection taught her valuable lessons about her craft and the publishing industry.

Learning from Setbacks

When confronted with challenges or setbacks in our lives, our initial response tends to be universal:

Complaining: We often find ourselves asking, "Why is this happening to us?" and Pondering: "What should I do now? It's over for me! This is unacceptable!"

It's normal to feel upset initially, but once that feeling fades, we all have a decision to make. We can either keep feeling bad and only think about the negatives, or we can look for something useful to learn from the problem. It's like when you face a tough day at work – you can either keep complaining about it, or you can figure out what you can improve or learn from the experience.

Certainly, we all go through uncertain or challenging times, but there's usually a positive aspect to the difficulty. What we label as a "problem" might not actually be a problem; it could be an opportunity. For example, a challenge might highlight a change we can make to enhance certain aspects of our life. Without facing the difficulty, we might never have taken the positive step towards improvement.

My father used to always narrate me a story where this man faced a rough patch in his career. He lost his job unexpectedly, leaving him feeling defeated and uncertain about the future. Initially disappointed, he could have dwelt on the negative aspects of the situation. However, he chose a different path.

During his period of unemployment, this man realised that he had a passion for entrepreneurship and had always dreamed of starting his own business. Losing his job became the opportunity he needed to pursue this dream. Instead of seeing it as a setback, he used the time to develop a business plan and acquire the necessary skills.

Listing these motivating stories from him during those days had no impact on me at that time.

But now, when I sit back and look at my own career, I find whatever happened to me happened for good.

To explain things better, consider a situation where, after giving a job interview, you were one hundred percent convinced that you would be selected. You waited for the selection letter to come, but it never arrived. Someone else was hired for that job. Maybe at that moment, you may have felt, "this is the end of it." Days later, another opportunity came, and you got selected. You realised that the previous position was much less desirable than the one that came later, and that the earlier rejection was, in fact, a blessing!

There is a very popular saying in our country that "if it is done according to your wish, then it is good, and if it is not done according to your wish, then it is even better," because then it is God's will. And there is no one who can think better than God for us.

Hope the concept is clear so far. Here in this chapter, we were talking about "Resilience." You will be surprised to know that Resilience involves learning from setbacks as well, using them as opportunities for growth.

Let's learn three ways in which setbacks can serve us:

1. Analysing Setbacks

Setbacks are valuable learning opportunities. Resilient individuals take the time to analyse their setbacks, identifying what went wrong and why.

They assess their actions, decisions, and strategies to gain insights, so that they can make informed decisions in the future.

2. Adapting and Iterating

Learning from setbacks involves making necessary adjustments and iterations. Resilient individuals do not dwell on past failures, but use them as stepping stones for improvement. They adapt their approaches, refine their strategies, and apply the lessons learned to future endeavours.

3. Maintaining Perspective

Maintaining perspective is crucial when learning from setbacks. Resilient individuals avoid negative thinking and recognise that setbacks are a natural part of any journey. They understand that, even the most successful people, have faced failures and challenges along the way.

Real-life examples showcase this process.

Real-Life Example 4: Thomas Edison

Background: Thomas Edison, one of history's greatest inventors, experienced numerous failures on his journey to success. He made thousands of unsuccessful attempts to create a practical electric light bulb.

Learning from Setbacks:

- Edison famously said, "I have not failed. I've just found 10,000 ways that won't work." He viewed each setback as a valuable lesson.
- His relentless experimentation eventually led to the creation of a long-lasting, practical light bulb.

Real-Life Example 5: SpaceX and Elon Musk

Background: SpaceX, the aerospace manufacturer and space transportation company founded by Elon Musk, faced multiple failures and setbacks, including rocket explosions and budget challenges.

Learning from Setbacks:

- SpaceX embraced each setback as an opportunity to improve its rockets and processes.
- They learned from their mistakes and went on to successfully launch and land reusable rockets, revolutionising space travel.

Conclusion

Adopting resilience is fundamental to achieving personal and professional success. Resilience provides the strength and determination needed to navigate life's complexities, overcome obstacles, and persevere in the face of adversity. By building resilience skills, individuals can enhance their ability to withstand setbacks and continue working toward their goals. Furthermore, learning from setbacks is a vital component of resilience as it allows individuals to grow stronger, wiser, and more prepared for future challenges.

Resilience is the key to turning adversity into success. Real-life examples like Oprah Winfrey, Nelson Mandela, J.K. Rowling, Thomas Edison, and SpaceX demonstrate the power of resilience in overcoming obstacles, building essential skills, and learning from setbacks. By developing positive thinking, adaptability, goal-setting, and building a support system, you can enhance your resilience and increase your capacity to achieve success, no matter the challenges you face. Remember, setbacks are not roadblocks; they are stepping stones on your journey to success.

— 4 —

Optimism: The Fuel of Achievement

Introduction

Optimism, often defined as a hopeful and positive outlook on life, plays a significant role in personal and professional success. Optimistic individuals tend to approach challenges with a sense of confidence, resilience, and a belief that they can overcome obstacles. In this chapter, we will explore the crucial role of optimism in achieving success, strategies for developing and nurturing optimism, and the transformative power of positive visualisation.

The Role of Optimism in Success

Optimism is the unwavering belief that success is not just possible, but likely, even in the face of challenges and setbacks. It acts as the driving force that propels individuals toward their goals.

1. Resilience in the Face of Adversity

Optimism is a key driver of resilience, the ability to bounce back from setbacks and adversity. Optimistic individuals are more likely to view failures as temporary and specific, rather than permanent and pervasive. This mindset enables them to persevere through difficult times and continue working toward their goals.

2. Motivation and Goal Achievement

Optimism serves as a powerful motivator. When individuals maintain a positive outlook, they are more likely to set ambitious goals and remain committed to achieving them. Optimistic people believe in their ability to make a difference and are more inclined to take action to realise their aspirations.

3. Improved Problem-Solving

Optimism is linked to enhanced problem-solving abilities. Optimistic individuals approach challenges with a problem-solving mindset, seeking solutions and viewing obstacles as opportunities for growth. This mindset fosters creativity and resourcefulness.

4. Enhanced Well-being

Optimism is associated with greater overall well-being. Optimistic individuals tend to experience lower levels of stress, improved physical health, and greater life satisfaction. Their positive outlook contributes to a higher quality of life.

Athletes often exemplify this role of optimism in the most inspiring ways.

Real-Life Example 1: Michael Jordan

Background: Michael Jordan, widely regarded as one of the greatest basketball players of all time, faced numerous obstacles throughout his career. His journey to success was marked by setbacks, including being cut from his high school basketball team.

Optimism and Success

Jordan's unwavering optimism was evident in his relentless work ethic and self-belief. He once said, *"I can accept failure; everyone fails at something,"* but I can't accept not trying." His optimism drove him to become a six-time NBA champion, five-time NBA MVP, and a global icon in the world of sports.

Strategies for Developing Optimism

Optimism is a mindset that can be cultivated and strengthened over time.

1. Cultivate Self-Awareness

Developing optimism begins with self-awareness. Pay attention to your thought patterns and identify any negative or pessimistic tendencies. Understanding how you typically respond to challenges is the first step in making positive changes.

2. Reframe Negative Thoughts

Practice cognitive reframing, a technique that involves challenging and changing negative thoughts. When faced with a setback, reframe your thinking by focusing on potential solutions, lessons learned, and the opportunities for growth that it presents.

3. Surround Yourself with Positivity

Surrounding yourself with optimistic and supportive individuals can be beneficial. Engage in conversations and relationships that promote positivity and encourage a hopeful outlook.

4. Practice Gratitude

Gratitude is a powerful tool for developing optimism. Regularly take time to reflect on the things you're grateful for. This practice can shift your focus from what is lacking in your life to what you appreciate, leading to a more optimistic perspective.

Athletes often employ specific strategies to nurture and harness their optimism.

Real-Life Example 2: Serena Williams,

Background: Serena Williams, one of the most dominant tennis players in history, has faced injuries, setbacks, and personal challenges during her career.

Strategies for Developing Optimism:

- Positive Self-talk: Serena consistently engages in positive self-talk, using phrases like *"I am strong,"* *"I am capable,"* and *"I can do this"* to boost her self-confidence.
- Visualisation: She visualises success on the court, imagining herself making perfect shots and winning crucial points.

The Power of Positive Visualisation

1. Visualisation Techniques

Positive visualisation involves mentally rehearsing successful outcomes and imagining the achievement of your goals. Visualisation techniques can help you build and sustain optimism by creating a mental picture of your desired future. This process enhances your belief that success is possible.

2. Setting Clear Goals

Before engaging in positive visualisation, it is essential to set clear and specific goals. Knowing precisely what you want to achieve allows you to visualise your path to success more effectively.

3. Visualisation Rituals

Incorporate positive visualisation into your daily routine. Spend a few minutes each day visualising your goals, imagining the steps you need to take, and enjoy the feeling of accomplishment. Consistency is key to maximising the benefits of this practice.

4. Harnessing the Law of Attraction

Positive visualisation aligns with the concept of the Law of Attraction, which suggests that focusing on positive thoughts and desires can attract corresponding positive outcomes. By consistently visualising your goals and maintaining an optimistic outlook, you can draw success towards you.

Visualisation is a powerful tool that athletes use to enhance their optimism and improve their performance. By vividly imagining themselves succeeding, they build confidence and focus.

Real-Life Example 3: Muhammad Ali

Background: Muhammad Ali, one of the most legendary boxers of all time, was known for his brash confidence and unwavering belief in his abilities. His optimism was a driving force behind his success.

The Power of Positive Visualisation:

- *Ali often visualised himself winning fights before they happened. He would describe his victories in great detail, even predicting the round in which he would win.*
- This positive visualisation not only boosted his confidence, but also influenced his opponents, making them doubt their own abilities.

Real-Life Example 4: The U.S. Women's National Soccer Team

Background: The U.S. Women's National Soccer Team is known for its consistent success on the international stage, winning multiple FIFA World Cup championships.

The Power of Positive Visualisation:

- The team practices positive visualisation collectively. Before each major tournament, they visualise themselves scoring goals, making key saves, and celebrating victories.
- This shared optimism and visualisation reinforce their belief in their abilities and their determination to win.

Conclusion

Optimism is a powerful force that motivates individuals toward achievement and success. It encourages resilience, motivation, problem-solving abilities, and overall well-being. Developing and nurturing optimism requires self-awareness, cognitive reframing, positive social connections, and the practice of gratitude. Additionally, positive visualisation is a transformative tool that can solidify your optimism and propel you closer to your goals. By holding optimism, you can unlock your full potential, face challenges with confidence, and turn your aspirations into reality.

Optimism is the fuel that ignites achievement, and athletes are living proof of its transformative power. Real-life examples like Michael Jordan, Serena Williams, Muhammad Ali, and the U.S. Women's National Soccer Team demonstrate how optimism drives success. By employing strategies such as positive self-talk, visualisation, and unwavering self-belief, athletes cultivate and harness their optimism, setting an inspiring example for all of us. The power of positive visualisation, in particular, is a tool that can help us build confidence and focus on our goals, no matter how challenging they may seem.

– 5 –

Self-Confidence: Your Greatest Asset

Self-confidence is a powerful psychological trait that plays a decisive role in one's personal and professional development. This chapter explores the profound connection between self-confidence and success, delves into strategies for building and maintaining self-confidence, and provides insights on overcoming self-doubt. It emphasises the importance of self-confidence as a fundamental asset for individuals striving to achieve their goals and fulfil their potential.

Introduction

Self-confidence is a psychological state characterised by a belief in one's abilities, worth, and potential for success. It serves as a foundational pillar in the pursuit of personal and professional achievements. Confidence, often regarded as an inner strength, can significantly influence the course of an individual's life. This chapter explores the complex relationship between self-confidence and success, offers practical guidance on building and nurturing self-confidence, and addresses the challenges posed by self-doubt.

The Connection Between Confidence and Success

1. Enhanced Performance: Self-confidence has a direct impact on performance. Individuals who believe in their abilities are more likely to set and strive for challenging goals, take calculated risks, and perform at their best. This positive self-perception fosters a sense of competence and resilience in the face of setbacks.

2. Positive Self-Presentation: Confidence is magnetic. Confident individuals tend to exude charisma and make favourable impressions on others. This can lead to better social and professional relationships, as well as increased opportunities for collaboration and advancement.

3. Resilience: Self-confidence acts as a shield against the effects of failure and criticism. Confident individuals are better equipped to bounce back from setbacks, learn from their mistakes, and remain firm in the face of any adversity.

4. Goal Achievement: Confidence serves as a driving force behind goal-setting and attainment. When individuals believe in their ability to succeed, they are more likely to set ambitious goals and pursue them with determination.

Let us further elaborate on the Power of Self-Confidence...

Self-confidence is often the differentiating factor between those who achieve success and those who fall short of their potential. It is the unwavering belief in your abilities, decisions, and judgements. Confidence is the driving force behind taking risks, capturing opportunities, and bouncing back from failures.

Real-Life Example 1: Usain Bolt

Background: Usain Bolt, the Jamaican sprinter often referred to as the "fastest man in the world," holds numerous world records and Olympic gold medals. He faced immense pressure to perform on the global stage.

Confidence and Success

Bolt's exceptional self-confidence was evident in his pre-race actions, such as pointing to himself as the clear winner before a race even began. This self-assuredness, almost an arrogance, allowed him to perform at his peak consistently, making him an Olympic legend.

Building Self-Confidence

Self-confidence is not an inherent trait, but a skill that can be cultivated and developed. Here are strategies to build and enhance self-confidence:

1. Self-Awareness: Begin by gaining a deep understanding of yourself, your strengths, and your areas for improvement. Self-awareness lays the foundation for realistic self-appraisal.

2. Set Realistic Goals: Set achievable, yet challenging goals that align with your abilities and aspirations. Success in smaller tasks can boost your confidence for more significant undertakings.

3. Positive Self-Talk: Replace negative self-talk with positive self-dialogues. Challenge and reframe self-limiting beliefs by focusing on your past successes and potential.

4. Competence Development: Invest time in acquiring new skills and honing existing ones. Gaining competence in various areas will naturally boost your confidence.

5. Visualise Success: Use visualisation techniques to imagine yourself succeeding in your endeavours. This mental rehearsal can boost your confidence and reduce anxiety.

6. Seek Feedback: Embrace constructive feedback as a tool for growth. Actively solicit feedback from mentors, peers, or supervisors to gain insights into areas of improvement.

Real-Life Example 2: Arnold Schwarzenegger

Background: Arnold Schwarzenegger, a bodybuilder, actor, and politician, achieved extraordinary success in multiple fields. However, his thick Austrian accent and unconventional background initially made him an unlikely Hollywood star.

Building Self-Confidence:

- Setting and Achieving Goals: Schwarzenegger set clear and ambitious goals in bodybuilding, acting, and politics. Achieving these goals built his confidence over time.

- Positive Self-talk: He practised positive self-talk and believed in the power of affirmations. Repeating phrases like "I can do it" and "I am the best" reinforced his self-confidence.

Overcoming Self-Doubt

To help individuals understand the nature of self-doubt and provide strategies to overcome it, build self-confidence, and achieve their goals.

Introduction

Self-doubt is a common and natural part of the human experience. At some point in our lives, we all experience moments of insecurity and uncertainty. However, self-doubt can become a significant barrier to personal growth, happiness, and success if not managed effectively. In this lesson, we will explore what self-doubt is, why it happens, and strategies to overcome it.

I. Understanding Self-Doubt

1. Defining Self-Doubt:

- Self-doubt is the lack of confidence in oneself and one's abilities. It can manifest as feelings of inadequacy, fear of failure, or a persistent belief that you are not good enough.

2. Causes of Self-Doubt:

- Comparison with others.
- Past failures or criticism.
- Fear of the unknown.
- Perfectionism.

3. Recognising Self-Doubt:

- Pay attention to the thoughts and feelings associated with self-doubt.
- Notice physical sensations like tension, anxiety, or a racing heart.

II. Strategies for Overcoming Self-Doubt

1. Practice Self-Awareness:

- Recognise when self-doubt is creeping in.
- Keep a journal to track your thoughts and emotions.

2. Challenge Negative Thoughts:

- Identify and challenge irrational or negative thoughts.

  Replace them with more realistic and positive affirmations.

3. Set Realistic Goals:

- Break down your larger goals into smaller, achievable steps.
- Celebrate your accomplishments along the way.

4. Embrace Failure:

- Understand that failure is a part of the learning process.
- Reframe failures as opportunities for growth and learning.

5. Practice Self-Compassion:

- Treat yourself with the same kindness and understanding you would offer a friend.
- Avoid self-criticism and self-judgement.

6. Seek Support:

- Talk to friends, family, or a therapist about your self-doubt.
- Surround yourself with positive and supportive individuals.

7. Develop Skills and Knowledge:

- Invest in self-improvement through education and skill-building.
- Increased competence can boost confidence.

8. Visualisation and Positive Self-Talk:

- Visualise your success and imagine yourself achieving your goals.
- Use positive self-talk to reinforce your belief in your abilities.

III. Building Lasting Self-Confidence

1. Set and Achieve Goals:

- Achieving your goals, even small ones, can boost your confidence.

2. Maintain a Growth Mindset:

- Embrace challenges as opportunities to grow and learn.
- Believe in your capacity to develop your abilities.

3. Celebrate Your Achievements:

- Recognise and reward yourself for your accomplishments.

4. Stay Resilient:

- Build the capacity to bounce back from setbacks and adversity.

Conclusion

Self-confidence is indeed your greatest asset on the path to success. Real-life examples like Usain Bolt, Arnold Schwarzenegger, Malala Yousafzai, Serena Williams, and J.K. Rowling illustrate the profound connection between self-confidence and success. By building self-confidence through goal-setting, positive self-talk, authenticity, and a supportive network, individuals can achieve their ambitions with unwavering belief in their abilities. Overcoming self-doubt, a common obstacle on the journey to self-confidence, requires mental toughness, perseverance, and the acceptance of imperfection. Ultimately, self-confidence empowers individuals to pursue their dreams, take calculated risks, and reach their full potential in any field or endeavour.

– 6 –

Positive Relationships: The Building Blocks of Success

Positive relationships are essential components of human well-being, providing emotional support, personal growth, and a sense of belonging. This chapter explores the profound importance of positive connections, offers insights on nurturing supportive relationships, and discusses strategies for handling negative influences to maintain a healthy social environment. Understanding the dynamics of positive relationships can enhance one's overall quality of life and foster personal development.

Introduction

Positive relationships are the heart and soul of human existence. They encompass connections with family, friends, romantic partners, colleagues, and the broader community. These connections play a pivotal role in shaping our emotions, thoughts, and behaviours. This chapter delves into the significance of positive relationships, provides guidance on cultivating them, and discusses strategies for mitigating the impact of negative influences within our social networks.

The Story of Meera

In a bustling city in India, where tradition and modernity coexisted, there lived a young woman named Meera. She was a prime example of how positive connections could shape a person's life in the Indian context.

Meera had grown up in a close-knit neighbourhood where her family had lived for generations. Her grandparents had always stressed the importance of maintaining strong relationships within the community, and she had absorbed this wisdom from an early age. She believed that these bonds were the foundations of Indian society.

Meera was known for her warm and inviting conduct. She greeted her neighbours with folded hands and a genuine smile, a tradition that resonated deeply with the people in her community. Her friendly nature made her a beloved figure in the neighbourhood.

One of Meera's closest friends was Raj, a middle-aged man who had lost his job due to a sudden downturn in the local economy. He struggled to make ends meet and was sinking into despair. Meera, however, refused to let him face his troubles alone. She introduced Raj to various job opportunities and helped him network within the community. With her support, Raj soon found a new job and regained his self-confidence.

Meera's ability to foster positive connections also had a significant impact on her family. When her younger brother, Arjun, faced difficulties in his studies, Meera encouraged him to seek guidance from a retired teacher in the neighbourhood. The elderly teacher, Mrs. Gupta, was more than willing to help, and under her mentorship, Arjun's grades improved significantly.

Meera's mother, Mrs. Sharma, was a skilled cook who had always dreamed of starting her own catering business. Meera, along with her close friend Priya, who was a talented event planner, helped turn that dream into a reality. Together, they created a thriving catering business that served authentic Indian cuisine. Meera's positive connections not only supported her family but also strengthened the community's economy.

One day, a severe flood hit the city, leaving hundreds of families homeless. Meera's community came together to help the victims, organising food drives and shelter for those in need. Meera's positive connections played a crucial role in this effort. Her warm relationships with her neighbours facilitated swift and effective aid for the flood victims.

As time passed, Meera's story of positive connections became an inspiration for others. People realised that these connections were not just about helping in times of need, but about fostering a sense of unity and togetherness in the Indian context. Meera's neighbourhood, once just a collection of houses, became a vibrant and compassionate community.

The importance of positive connections in the Indian context was evident through Meera's life. These relationships served as a support system, fostering personal and collective growth. They were a testament to the idea that, in India, building and maintaining positive connections was not just a social custom, but a way to create a harmonious and thriving society, one that celebrated the spirit of "Vasudhaiva Kutumbakam" – the world is one family.

The Importance of Positive Connections

1. Emotional Well-being: Positive relationships contribute significantly to emotional health. They offer a source of comfort, validation, and empathy during challenging times, reducing stress and enhancing overall well-being.

2. Personal Growth: Supportive relationships provide opportunities for personal growth and self-discovery. Constructive feedback and encouragement from trusted individuals can facilitate self-improvement and self-actualisation.

3. Sense of Belonging: Humans have an innate need to belong. Positive relationships satisfy this need by creating a sense of community and connectedness, reducing feelings of isolation and loneliness.

4. Improved Mental and Physical Health: Studies show that individuals with strong social ties tend to enjoy better mental and physical health outcomes. Positive relationships can help in

coping with illnesses and mitigating the effects of stress.

Imagine a world without positive relationships – a world where support, encouragement, and collaboration are absent. Such a world would be isolating, discouraging, and devoid of the opportunities that arise from connecting with others. In this chapter, we explore the vital role that positive relationships play in achieving success, using a unique story to illustrate their profound impact.

The Story of Maria and Sarah

Maria, a talented young entrepreneur, had a vision to launch a sustainable fashion brand that would make a positive impact on the environment. Her dream was ambitious, and the road to success seemed long and challenging. However, Maria was not alone in her journey.

Enter Sarah, an experienced fashion industry professional, who shared Maria's passion for sustainability. They met at a networking event and instantly connected over their shared vision. Sarah offered Maria valuable insights, introduced her to key industry contacts, and provided guidance on navigating the fashion world.

With Sarah's support and mentorship, Maria's sustainable fashion brand flourished. What started as a small startup grew into a thriving business that not only achieved financial success but also made a significant contribution to environmental sustainability.

Maria's story illustrates the importance of positive connections in the pursuit of success. Whether in entrepreneurship, academia, sports, or any field, nurturing supportive relationships can be a game-changer.

Nurturing Supportive Relationships

This is a story of a woman named Maya. She was a true master of nurturing supportive relationships and believed that these bonds were the cornerstone of personal growth and success. Her story was a testament to the power of these connections and the strategies she used to cultivate them.

Maya's journey began when she joined a small marketing firm called BrightPath Solutions. Her first day was filled with excitement and apprehension, but she was determined to make a difference. She quickly realised that nurturing supportive relationships would be the key to her success.

Strategy 1: Active Listening and Empathy

Maya had a colleague named Michael, who was known for his expertise in marketing strategy. Instead of being intimidated, she approached him with humility and genuine curiosity to learn from his experience. She actively listened to his insights and empathised with his challenges. Michael, in turn, was impressed by Maya's willingness to understand and connect with him. This marked the beginning of a mentorship that would help her grow in her career.

Strategy 2: Offering Support

As Maya worked on her projects, she encountered several challenges. Rather than keeping her struggles to herself, she reached out to her coworkers for help. She offered her support to them as well, creating a sense of camaraderie. This spirit of collaboration, not only solved problems, but also strengthened the bonds within the team.

Strategy 3: Gratitude and Recognition

Maya knew the importance of recognising the efforts of her colleagues. She regularly expressed gratitude for their contributions, whether big or small. This simple act of acknowledgement made her coworkers feel valued and appreciated. In return, they reciprocated with their support, knowing that Maya was a true team player.

Strategy 4: Consistency and Trustworthiness

Maya was dependable. Her colleagues knew they could rely on her, and she delivered on her promises consistently. Her trustworthiness became a cornerstone of her relationships, making her an invaluable member of the team.

Over time, Maya's career soared. She was known not only for her skills but also for her ability to nurture supportive relationships within the company. Her story was a testament to how these strategies could lead to personal growth and success.

Outside of work, Maya extended these strategies to her personal life. She was an active member of her community, always ready to lend a helping hand and offering support to her friends and neighbours. She believed that the same principles applied beyond the workplace, and these relationships enriched her life in countless ways.

Maya's story became an inspiration, not only within her company, but also in her community. Her journey emphasised the importance of building and maintaining positive relationships as a powerful tool for personal growth and success. It proved that in a fast-paced world, the ability to connect, collaborate, and support others was the key to achieving one's goals and fostering a more compassionate and prosperous society. Maya's legacy was a testament to the enduring power of nurturing supportive relationships.

Building and maintaining positive relationships is an essential skill that can lead to personal growth and success. Here are strategies for nurturing supportive relationships:

1. Effective Communication: Open and honest communication forms the bedrock of healthy relationships. Actively listen to others, express your feelings and needs clearly, and seek understanding, rather than judgement.

2. Empathy and Compassion: Practice empathy by understanding and sharing the emotions of others. Show compassion by offering support and kindness when needed, without judgement.

3. Quality Time: Spend quality time with loved ones. Engage in activities that foster bonding and create memorable experiences.

4. Conflict Resolution: Conflicts are a natural part of any relationship. Develop conflict resolution skills to address disagreements constructively, focusing on finding mutually acceptable solutions.

5. Boundaries: Establish and communicate personal boundaries to ensure that your relationships remain healthy and respectful. Boundaries define what is acceptable behaviour within the relationship.

Real-Life Example 1: Bill Gates and Warren Buffett

Background: Bill Gates, co-founder of Microsoft, and Warren Buffett, one of the world's most successful investors, developed a deep friendship over the years.

Nurturing Supportive Relationships:

- Shared Values: Both Gates and Buffett share a commitment to philanthropy. Their shared values brought them closer together.

- Regular Communication: Despite their busy schedules, they make time for regular conversations, fostering a strong bond.

Real-Life Example 2: Tim Cook and Steve Jobs

Background: Tim Cook, the current CEO of Apple, had a close professional and personal relationship with the late Steve Jobs, Apple's co-founder.

Nurturing Supportive Relationships:

- Complementary Skills: Cook's operational expertise complemented Jobs' creative genius. Their collaboration was essential to Apple's success.
- Respect and Trust: They shared mutual respect and trust, which allowed them to navigate challenges and make critical decisions.

Handling Negative Influences

Handling negative influences in our relationships is a critical aspect of personal growth and success. Let's explore a story that highlights this important dimension:

In the vibrant city of Mumbai, where dreams and ambitions thrived, there lived a young woman named Reshmi. She was determined to make a name for herself in the world of art. Reshmi was not a novice to the idea that not all relationships were positive, and she understood the importance of handling negative influences.

The Unsupportive Friend

Reshmi had a close friend named Sarah who had always been sceptical about her artistic occupation. Sarah often questioned Reshmi's career choice, doubting that she could achieve success as an artist. At first, Reshmi was disheartened by Sarah's negativity, but she realised that she needed to address the issue.

Strategy 1: Setting Boundaries

Reshmi sat down with Sarah for an honest conversation. She explained her dreams and the importance of Sarah's support. Reshmi set clear boundaries, making it known that she needed friends who believed in her ambitions. This conversation helped Sarah understand the impact of her negativity, and over time, she began to show more support.

The Overbearing Relative

Reshmi also faced a challenge in her family. Her uncle, a successful businessman, believed that art was an impractical career. He often shared stories of artists who had struggled financially. Reshmi knew she had to address this negative influence as well.

Strategy 2: Open Communication

Instead of avoiding the topic, Reshmi decided to have a candid conversation with her uncle. She explained her passion for art and her determination to succeed. Reshmi's confidence and conviction left an impression on her uncle. He realised that she was dedicated to her craft and began to offer advice and support, rather than criticism.

The Toxic Colleague

At her art studio, Reshmi encountered a fellow artist who was competitive and often tried to undermine her work. This negative influence was particularly challenging because it affected her professional life.

Strategy 3: Focusing on Self-Growth

Reshmi decided not to engage in a rivalry with the fellow artist. Instead, she focused on improving her skills and building her portfolio. Over time, her dedication and success spoke for themselves, and she gained recognition in the art community. The fellow artist's negative influence gradually lost its power.

Through these experiences, Reshmi learned that handling negative influences was equally important in her journey to success. She realised that setting boundaries, engaging in open communication, and focusing on her own growth were valuable strategies. Reshmi also understood that not every relationship needed to be severed; sometimes, by addressing the negativity, she could transform it into a more positive and supportive force.

Reshmi's story became an inspiration for others. Her ability to handle negative influences and turn them into stepping stones towards her success emphasised the importance of not only nurturing positive relationships, but also managing and redirecting the negative ones. In doing so, Reshmi showed that personal growth and success were not only about achieving dreams, but also about mastering the art of handling life's challenges.

So, to reiterate... not all relationships are positive, and sometimes negative influences can hinder your path to success. Learning to handle such influences is equally important.

1. Recognise Toxic Relationships: Be vigilant in identifying toxic or negative influences in your life. These relationships can drain your energy and hinder personal growth.
2. Set Healthy Boundaries: When dealing with negative influences, establish and enforce clear boundaries. Limit the time and emotional energy you invest in these relationships.
3. Seek Support: Talk to a trusted friend or a mental health professional for guidance and support when dealing with toxic relationships. They can provide valuable perspectives and strategies.
4. Limit Exposure: Minimise exposure to negative individuals or situations when possible. Surround yourself with positive influences that uplift and inspire you.

Real-Life Example 3: Serena Williams

Background: Serena Williams, a tennis legend, has faced criticism and negative comments throughout her career, often related to her appearance and race.

Handling Negative Influences:

- Resilience: Serena focused on her game and success, using negative comments as motivation to prove her critics wrong.
- Support System: She leaned on her family and friends for emotional support, allowing her to rise above negativity.

Real-Life Example 4: Michael Jordan

Background: Michael Jordan, a basketball icon, faced challenges from teammates who questioned his leadership style.

Handling Negative Influences:

- Leading by Example: Jordan responded by setting high standards through his work ethic and dedication, earning the respect of his teammates.
- Selective Influence: He chose to surround himself with individuals who shared his commitment to success, minimising the impact of negative influences.

Conclusion

Positive relationships are the cornerstone of personal and professional success. The story of Maria and Sarah, along with real-life examples of Bill Gates, Warren Buffett, Tim Cook, Steve Jobs, Serena Williams, and Michael Jordan, illustrates the profound impact of supportive connections. Nurturing these relationships through shared values, regular communication, and mutual respect can provide invaluable guidance, support, and opportunities on your journey to success.

Moreover, learning to handle negative influences with resilience, selective influence, and a strong support system is equally crucial. Positive relationships empower individuals to overcome obstacles, pursue their dreams, and thrive in a world where collaboration and connection are the keys to unlocking their full potential.

– 7 –

Goal-Setting and Persistence

Setting and achieving goals are fundamental aspects of personal and professional growth. This chapter explores the process of setting SMART (Specific, Measurable, Achievable, Relevant, Time-bound) goals, discusses the art of perseverance in pursuing these goals, and offers strategies for overcoming obstacles that may arise along the way. By mastering the art of goal-setting and persistence, individuals can unlock their full potential and achieve their aspirations.

Introduction

Goal-setting and persistence are intrinsically linked to human achievement. Goals provide direction, motivation, and a framework for personal and professional growth. Perseverance, on the other hand, is the unwavering commitment and determination to overcome obstacles and setbacks on the path to goal attainment. This chapter delves into the process of setting SMART goals, explores the art of perseverance, and discusses strategies for surmounting obstacles in the pursuit of one's objectives.

Setting SMART Goals

Setting SMART (Specific, Measurable, Achievable, Relevant, Time-bound) goals is a universal approach to achieving success.

1. Specific: Goals should be clearly defined and specific. Ambiguity can lead to confusion and a lack of focus. By specifying exactly what you want to achieve, you provide a clear target.

2. Measurable: Goals must be measurable to track progress and determine when you have successfully achieved them. Quantify your objectives whenever possible.

3. Achievable: Ensure that your goals are realistic and attainable. While ambition is admirable, setting unattainable goals can lead to frustration and disappointment.

4. Relevant: Goals should align with your values and long-term objectives. Ensure that they are relevant to your overall mission and aspirations.

5. Time-bound: Set a deadline for your goals. Having a timeframe creates a sense of urgency and helps you prioritise your efforts.

In the Indian subcontinent, individuals from various backgrounds have demonstrated the power of setting such goals with precision.

Real-Life Example 1: Dr. APJ Abdul Kalam

Background: Dr APJ Abdul Kalam, a renowned Indian scientist and former President of India, had a visionary goal to strengthen India's aerospace capabilities.

Setting SMART Goals:

- Specific (1980): In 1980, Kalam proposed the development of India's own satellite launch vehicle (SLV) to put satellites into orbit.
- Measurable (1980-1983): Over the next three years, he and his team at ISRO (Indian Space Research Organisation) worked diligently to achieve a series of milestones, including successful static tests of the SLV's engine.
- Achievable (1980-1983): The team at ISRO tackled the project with meticulous planning, breaking it down into achievable stages.
- Relevant (1980): Kalam's goal was profoundly relevant to India's strategic and technological advancement during a pivotal period.
- Time-Bound (1983): Kalam set a clear timeline, aiming for a launch by 1983.

The Art of Perseverance

1. Resilience: Develop resilience to bounce back from setbacks and failures. Understand that setbacks are part of the journey and opportunities for growth.

2. Maintain Focus: Stay focused on your goals, even when faced with distractions or competing priorities. Regularly remind yourself of your objectives to maintain motivation.

3. Adaptability: Be open to adapting your strategies when necessary. Sometimes, the path to your goal may require adjustments based on new information or circumstances.

4. Self-Discipline: Cultivate self-discipline to stay committed to your goals, especially when the initial enthusiasm wanes. Consistent effort is key to persistence.

5. Seek Support: Surround yourself with a support system of friends, mentors, or coaches who can offer guidance, encouragement, and accountability.

Perseverance is a deeply ingrained value in the Indian subcontinent, where individuals have historically faced adversity with unwavering determination.

Real-Life Example 2: Milkha Singh

Background: Milkha Singh, known as the "Flying Sikh," faced numerous challenges while aspiring to become an Olympic athlete.

The Art of Perseverance:

- Specific (1958): In 1958, Milkha Singh's goal was to compete in the 1960 Rome Olympics as a sprinter representing India.
- Measurable (1958-1960): Over the next two years, he endured gruelling training and competitions to meet the qualification standards.
- Achievable (1958-1960): Despite setbacks and injuries, Singh remained committed to achieving his goal.
- Relevant (1958): His goal was highly relevant to his passion for athletics and representing his nation on the world stage.
- Time-Bound (1960): The Rome Olympics in 1960 served as a clear deadline for his goal.

Real-Life Example 3: Ratan Tata

Background: Ratan Tata, a prominent Indian industrialist, demonstrated the art of perseverance while leading the Tata Group, a vast conglomerate with diverse business interests.

The Art of Perseverance:

- Specific (1991): In 1991, during a time of economic liberalisation in India, Tata aimed to transform the Tata Group into a globally competitive conglomerate.
- Measurable (1991-present): Over the decades, Tata spearheaded numerous acquisitions and expansions to enhance the group's global presence.
- Achievable (1991-present): Tata navigated complex regulatory landscapes and economic challenges with strategic decision-making.
- Relevant (1991): His goal was highly relevant to the Tata Group's legacy and future growth.
- Time-Bound (Ongoing): The ongoing journey of the Tata Group reflects the time-bound nature of Tata's vision.

Overcoming Obstacles

There is an old saying: *"If you want to be successful, you must be willing to be uncomfortable."*

This is so true!

If we have to achieve our goals and reach the pinnacle of our dreams, then we must confront our fears and obstacles.

This may sound simple, but most of us, in our lives, when faced with frightening or challenging situations, don't take any action; rather, we shy away from problems with fear of failure.

I am sure you will correlate yourself with this situation,

How many of us, with the fear of public speaking, never dared to stand on the podium?

How many of us, with the fear of getting embarrassed, never asked questions in schools, colleges, or meetings?

How many of us, with the fear of getting rejected, never applied for any competition?

How many of us, with the fear that the boss may not like the presentation, never prepared any PPT?

I am sure the number will be in millions, and they carry the same fear that you have, which is "FAILURE."

Let me explain this concept through my own story.

I used to speak very quickly since childhood. From class 1st to class 8th, I don't know what happened, but I started stammering.

Now I was scared of talking to people. Being in school, our teacher used to make us do book-reading in front of the whole class. Whenever my turn for book-reading came, I would tremble with fear.

The only thought that would come to my mind was that my friends in the class would laugh at me. Because my school was in a co-ed one, I thought girls would laugh at me. How would I be able to do book-reading because I am a stammerer?

So, I started making excuses of a headache and stomach ache to avoid my chance of book-reading.

I felt helpless and frustrated because I couldn't do book-reading in class, and unknowingly, my morale started falling.

However, while singing on stage during Annual Functions in front of the whole school, I was always a confident boy, winning solo song competitions and receiving accolades for the school during inter-school competitions.

My father, who was my best friend and mentor, observed this complexity and recommended a few actions that worked for me.

This is what he suggested

Keep yourself calm and relaxed before any public speech.

Do not try to speak many words at a time...

Speak slowly and don't rush to complete a thought. Take time to finish a sentence.

Take proper breath between your sentences and words!

And always maintain eye contact with your listeners...

So, what my father actually did was... he identified the problem, suggested certain methods and measures, gave me courage, and advised me to be resilient... and it all worked for me.

So, if someone like me can overcome his stammering and can now confidently speak, so can you.

We all can overcome our obstacles if we scientifically and meticulously follow the following:

1. Identify Challenges: Recognise potential obstacles that may impede your progress. Awareness is the first step in finding solutions.

2. Problem-Solving Skills: Develop effective problem-solving skills to address challenges systematically. Break down complex issues into manageable steps.

3. Adversity as Learning: View obstacles as opportunities for learning and growth. Each challenge you overcome enhances your resilience and problem-solving abilities.

4. Maintain a Positive Mindset: Maintain a positive attitude, even when facing difficulties. A positive mindset can boost your confidence and motivation.

5. Flexible Planning: Be willing to adjust your plans when obstacles arise. Flexibility allows you to adapt and find alternative routes to your goals.

Overcoming obstacles is a defining characteristic of individuals in the Indian subcontinent, and their stories resonate with determination and resilience.

Real-Life Example 4: Mary Kom

Background: Mary Kom, an Indian boxer, overcame societal and financial challenges while pursuing her passion for boxing.

Overcoming Obstacles:

– Specific (1999): In 1999, Kom set her sights on becoming a world-class boxer and representing India on the global stage.

- Measurable (1999-2000): Over the next year, she honed her skills and competed in international tournaments, measuring her progress.
- Achievable (1999-2000): Despite limited resources and societal barriers, Kom persevered and became a world champion boxer.
- Relevant (1999): Her goal was deeply relevant to her passion for boxing and bringing glory to India.
- Time-Bound (2000): Kom's goal was realised in the 2000 Women's World Amateur Boxing Championships, where she won her first gold medal.

Real-Life Example 5: Dhirubhai Ambani

Background: Dhirubhai Ambani, a visionary Indian entrepreneur, faced numerous obstacles while building the Reliance Group, one of India's largest conglomerates.

Overcoming Obstacles:

- Specific (1966): In 1966, Dhirubhai Ambani founded Reliance with the specific goal of making it a global business powerhouse.
- Measurable (1966-present): Over the decades, he navigated economic challenges, government regulations, and competition, while steadily expanding Reliance.

- Achievable (1966-present): His relentless pursuit of his goal, combined with innovative business strategies, allowed Reliance to thrive.
- Relevant (1966): His goal was profoundly relevant to his vision for the conglomerate's growth.
- Time-Bound (Ongoing): The ongoing success of Reliance Group is a testament to the time-bound nature of Ambani's vision.

Conclusion

Goal-setting and perseverance are universal principles, but the examples from the Indian subcontinent highlight their enduring relevance. Dr. APJ Abdul Kalam's pursuit of India's space capabilities, Milkha Singh's journey from adversity to athletic excellence, Ratan Tata's leadership in the corporate world, Mary Kom's rise to boxing stardom, and Dhirubhai Ambani's transformation of Reliance Group exemplify these principles.

These real-life examples underscore the significance of setting SMART goals, the art of perseverance in the face of adversity, and the ability to overcome obstacles with unwavering determination. These traits are not only applicable in the Indian subcontinent but also serve as inspirational stories for individuals striving for success in any part of the world.

– 8 –

The Role of Adaptability

Embracing Change

Adaptability is a crucial trait that enables individuals to navigate the complexities of life successfully. In this chapter, we will explore the significant role of adaptability in personal and professional growth. We'll discuss how embracing change, demonstrating flexibility in the face of challenges, and turning adversity into opportunity are all essential aspects of adaptability.

Adaptability is the ability to adjust to new conditions and circumstances, and it is a critical trait in today's rapidly changing world. Embracing change is the first step in harnessing the power of adaptability. Whether in personal life, business, or any endeavour, the capacity to welcome change with an open mind is key to success.

1. The Nature of Change

Change is an inevitable and constant aspect of life. Embracing change is the first step towards adaptability. It involves recognising that change is a natural part of the human experience and choosing to approach it with an open and positive mindset.

2. Overcoming Resistance

Resistance to change is a common response, driven by fear of the unknown or a desire for stability. However, embracing change allows individuals to grow and develop in response to new circumstances. Overcoming resistance involves acknowledging these fears and actively working to address them.

3. Continual Learning

Adaptability requires a commitment to continual learning and personal development. Embracing change means seeking out opportunities for growth and expansion, even when they seem challenging or uncomfortable.

The Transformative Power of Change

Specific (2020): The COVID-19 pandemic, which began in 2020, forced individuals and businesses worldwide to adapt to new realities, including remote work, travel restrictions, and shifting consumer behaviours.

Measurable (2020-present): The pandemic's impact is measurable through shifts in business models, remote work statistics and changes in consumer preferences.

Achievable (2020-present): Organisations adapted by implementing remote work policies, diversifying revenue streams, and accelerating digital transformation efforts.

Relevant (2020): Adapting to the pandemic was profoundly relevant to the survival and sustainability of businesses, and the well-being of individuals.

Time-Bound (Ongoing): Adapting to the post-pandemic world remains an ongoing process, as individuals and organisations continue to adjust.

Flexibility in the Face of Challenges

Flexibility is a key component of adaptability. It allows individuals and organisations to respond effectively to unforeseen challenges and pivot when necessary.

1. Responding to Unexpected Situations

Flexibility is the ability to respond effectively to unexpected situations or shifting circumstances. In the face of challenges, flexible individuals remain calm, assess the situation, and adjust their strategies as needed. They do not become rigid or overwhelmed when things don't go as planned.

2. Adapting to Diverse Environments

In today's interconnected world, adaptability is especially important. Individuals who can adapt to different cultures, work environments, and social situations are more likely to succeed in various aspects of life. Flexibility allows for smoother transitions and better relationships with others.

3. Resilience and Mental Well-being

Flexibility is closely tied to resilience and mental well-being. Flexible individuals are better equipped to handle stress and adversity as they can quickly adapt their thinking and behaviour to cope with challenging situations. This resilience contributes to better mental health outcomes.

Real-Life Example 1: Netflix

Background: Netflix began as a DVD rental service but transitioned into a streaming giant, reshaping the entertainment industry.

Flexibility in the Face of Challenges:

When streaming services disrupted the DVD rental market, Netflix pivoted to focus on streaming, capitalising on changing consumer preferences.

- The company's flexibility allowed it to not only survive, but also dominate the streaming market.

Real-Life Example 2: Amul

Background: Amul, an Indian dairy cooperative, faced challenges in the early 20th century, including milk surplus and unstable milk prices.

Flexibility in the Face of Challenges:

- Amul introduced the cooperative model, allowing farmers to have a stake in the business and share profits.
- This flexibility transformed Amul into one of the largest dairy companies globally.

Turning Adversity into Opportunity

Adversity often presents opportunities for growth and innovation.

1. Viewing Setbacks as Learning Experiences

One of the most significant aspects of adaptability is the ability to turn adversity into opportunity. Instead of seeing setbacks as failures, adaptable individuals view them as valuable learning experiences. They seek to understand what went wrong and how they can use this knowledge to improve in the future.

2. Pivoting and Innovation

Adaptability is closely linked to innovation. In both personal and professional contexts, adaptable individuals are more likely to pivot when circumstances change. They find creative solutions to problems, explore new possibilities, and adapt their strategies to capitalise on emerging opportunities.

3. Building Resilience

Adaptability strengthens resilience. When individuals consistently navigate challenges and uncertainties, they become more resilient over time. This resilience, in turn, enhances their capacity to adapt to future challenges and setbacks.

Those who can see the silver lining in difficult situations can thrive, even in the face of adversity.

Real-Life Example 3: SpaceX

Background: SpaceX, led by Elon Musk, experienced multiple failures in its early attempts to develop reusable rockets.

Turning Adversity into Opportunity:

- Musk viewed failures as opportunities to learn and improve rocket technology.
- SpaceX's ability to bounce back from setbacks ultimately led to the development of the Falcon 9, revolutionising space travel.

Real-Life Example 4: Alibaba

Background: Alibaba faced challenges during the dot-com bubble burst in the early 2000s, when many e-commerce companies collapsed.

Turning Adversity into Opportunity:

- Alibaba survived by pivoting into the business-to-business (B2B) market, connecting Chinese manufacturers with global buyers.
- This shift allowed Alibaba to weather the storm and become a global e-commerce giant.

Conclusion

Adaptability is a dynamic and multifaceted trait that empowers individuals to thrive in a rapidly changing world. By embracing change, demonstrating flexibility in the face of challenges, and turning adversity into opportunity, individuals can harness the full potential of adaptability. This trait not only enhances personal growth and well-being but also paves the way for success in both personal and professional spheres. Embracing adaptability as a guiding principle can lead to a more fulfilling and resilient life.

Adaptability is a hallmark of success in the modern world, and it plays a pivotal role in navigating change, demonstrating flexibility, and turning adversity into opportunity.

The transformative power of change, as seen through the lens of the COVID-19 pandemic, showcases the relevance and time-bound nature of adaptability.

Flexibility, exemplified by companies like Netflix and Amul, demonstrates how responding effectively to challenges can lead to success. Lastly, the ability to turn adversity into opportunity, as demonstrated by SpaceX and Alibaba, underscores the capacity of individuals and organisations to thrive in the face of setbacks.

Embracing adaptability as a core value can empower individuals and organisations to not only survive but also thrive in an ever-changing world. By welcoming change, remaining flexible, and seeing opportunities in adversity, individuals can unlock their full potential and achieve success in any field or endeavour.

– 9 –

Mindfulness and Emotional Intelligence

Introduction

Mindfulness and emotional intelligence are two essential components of personal and professional growth. In this chapter, we will explore how mindfulness can enhance emotional intelligence and contribute to success. We'll delve into the process of developing emotional intelligence and discuss how it aids in managing stress and emotions effectively.

Mindfulness in Achieving Success

1. Understanding Mindfulness

Mindfulness is the practice of being fully present in the moment, without judgement. It involves paying attention to thoughts, feelings, sensations, and the environment. Mindfulness encourages self-awareness and the ability to respond thoughtfully, rather than react impulsively.

2. The Role of Mindfulness in Success

Mindfulness is a powerful tool for achieving success. It enhances focus, decision-making, and problem-solving abilities. By cultivating mindfulness, individuals can approach challenges with a clear and calm mind, enabling them to make more effective choices and persevere through difficult situations.

3. Enhancing Creativity

Mindfulness fosters creativity by allowing individuals to tap into their inner resources and explore novel solutions. By quieting the mind and reducing mental clutter, mindfulness provides space for innovative thinking and fresh perspectives.

EXAMPLE

In the awe-inspiring world of space exploration, the Indian Space Research Organisation (ISRO) has consistently demonstrated that success is not merely about reaching the stars, but also about being deeply present in every moment of the journey. Mindfulness, the practice of being fully engaged in the present, has played a pivotal role in ISRO's remarkable success story, from the inception of its space missions to its latest lunar endeavour.

The Importance of Mindfulness

Specific (2023): In 2023, ISRO launched its highly anticipated Chandrayaan-3 mission, which aimed to build upon the successes of its predecessors and further explore the Moon's mysteries. Mindfulness was specific to ensuring the success of Chandrayaan-3, encompassing meticulous planning, rigorous testing, and the ability to stay fully engaged in the mission's various phases.

Measurable (2023): The impact of mindfulness in the Chandrayaan-3 mission can be measured through the successful launch, precise lunar orbit insertion, and the collection of valuable data that advances our understanding of the Moon.

Achievable (2023): Mindfulness was achievable through ISRO's unwavering commitment to continuous learning, rigorous training, and the development of innovative technologies.

Relevant (2023): Mindfulness was highly relevant to Chandrayaan-3's objectives of lunar exploration and scientific discovery.

Time-Bound (Ongoing): Mindfulness remains an ongoing practice within ISRO, guiding its missions to the Moon, Mars, and beyond.

Developing Emotional Intelligence

1. Understanding Emotional Intelligence

Emotional intelligence (EI) refers to the ability to recognise, understand, manage, and navigate one's own emotions and the emotions of others effectively. It involves empathy, self-awareness, and strong interpersonal skills.

2. The Link Between Mindfulness and Emotional Intelligence

Mindfulness and emotional intelligence are closely connected. Mindfulness practices can improve self-awareness, emotional regulation, and empathy, the core components of emotional intelligence. By being present and nonjudgmental, individuals can gain a deeper understanding of their emotions and those of others.

3. Developing Emotional Intelligence

To develop emotional intelligence:

- Self-awareness: Practice mindfulness to become more in tune with your emotions. Regularly check in with yourself to understand your feelings and reactions.

- Self-regulation: Use mindfulness techniques to manage your emotional responses. When you feel strong emotions, pause, breathe, and consider your actions before reacting.
- Empathy: Mindfulness fosters empathy by helping you become a more attentive listener and observer. Put yourself in others' shoes, and try to understand their perspectives.
- Social skills: Mindfulness can enhance your ability to communicate and collaborate effectively. Being fully present in conversations and practicing active listening can strengthen your social skills.

EXAMPLE

Emotional intelligence (EQ) is a cornerstone of ISRO's success in space exploration, underpinning its ability to foster collaboration, navigate complex challenges and manage the emotions that come with high-stakes missions.

Real-Life Example 1: Mars Orbiter Mission (Mangalyaan)

Background: ISRO's Mars Orbiter Mission (Mangalyaan), launched in 2013, was a historic endeavour to explore the Red Planet.

Developing Emotional Intelligence:

- The mission's success relied on the emotional intelligence of ISRO scientists and engineers who worked harmoniously across disciplines.
- Their ability to manage stress, stay composed during critical manoeuvres, and celebrate achievements, contributed to Mangalyaan's success.

Real-Life Example 2: Chandrayaan-2

Background: ISRO's Chandrayaan-2 mission, launched in 2019, aimed for a soft landing on the Moon's south polar region.

Developing Emotional Intelligence:

- The mission faced a setback during the lunar landing attempt. ISRO scientists and engineers displayed emotional intelligence by maintaining optimism, learning from the experience, and preparing for future missions, including Chandrayaan-3.

Managing Stress and Emotions

1. Stress Reduction

Mindfulness is a powerful stress management tool. By practicing mindfulness meditation, individuals can reduce the physiological and psychological effects of stress. Mindfulness helps break the cycle of rumination and worry, leading to a more relaxed state of mind.

2. Emotion Regulation

Mindfulness promotes better emotion regulation. When faced with strong emotions, individuals can use mindfulness techniques, such as deep breathing and grounding exercises, to stay grounded and make thoughtful choices, rather than reacting impulsively.

3. Cultivating Resilience

Mindfulness enhances resilience by helping individuals develop a more adaptive response to adversity. Instead of dwelling on difficulties, individuals can use mindfulness to accept challenges and bounce back more quickly.

EXAMPLE

Space missions are inherently demanding, with complex technical challenges and the potential for high-stress situations. Effective stress management and emotional control are vital for mission success.

Real-Life Example 3, Aditya-L1 Mission

Background: ISRO's upcoming Aditya-L1 mission, set to launch in the near future, aims to study the Sun.

Managing Stress and Emotions:

- As anticipation builds for this mission, ISRO scientists and engineers will face the stress of precise mission planning, launch preparations, and scientific data analysis.
- The ability to manage stress and maintain composure will be crucial for its success.

Conclusion

Mindfulness and emotional intelligence are integral to achieving success and fostering personal growth. Mindfulness cultivates self-awareness, reduces stress, and enhances creativity. When combined with emotional intelligence, individuals become better equipped to manage their emotions, understand others, and build meaningful relationships. The integration of mindfulness and emotional intelligence not only contributes to success but also promotes overall well-being and fulfillment in both personal and professional life. By embracing these practices, individuals can unlock their full potential and lead more balanced, resilient, and successful lives.

ISRO's space odyssey, marked by mindfulness, emotional intelligence, and effective stress management, is a testament to the organisation's unwavering commitment to pushing the boundaries of human knowledge. From Chandrayaan-1 to Chandrayaan-2, from the Mars Orbiter Mission to the forthcoming Aditya-L1 mission, ISRO's journey has been defined by innovation, collaboration, and resilience.

Mindfulness ensures that every aspect of ISRO's missions is executed with precision, from rocket design to telemetry analysis. Emotional intelligence fosters teamwork, communication, and adaptability, enabling multidisciplinary teams to navigate the challenges of space exploration. Managing stress and emotions empowers ISRO's scientists and engineers to persevere in the face of setbacks and continue their quest to unlock the mysteries of the cosmos.

As ISRO continues its mission to explore the Moon, the Sun, and beyond, the practice of mindfulness and the development of emotional intelligence will remain at the heart of its success, inspiring not only the scientific community, but all of humanity, to reach for the stars.

– 10 –
Cultivating Gratitude

Introduction

Gratitude, often defined as the appreciation of what is valuable and meaningful in life, is a powerful mindset that can lead to greater success and well-being. In this chapter, we will explore the profound connection between gratitude and success, discuss strategies for practicing gratitude on a daily basis, and explore how shifting one's perspective can lead to a more grateful and fulfilling life.

The Gratitude-Success Connection

1. Gratitude as a Success Catalyst

Gratitude is a catalyst for success because it cultivates a positive and optimistic mindset. When individuals focus on what they are grateful for, they tend to be more optimistic, which, in turn, leads to increased motivation, resilience, and overall well-being.

2. Improved Mental Health

Gratitude is linked to improved mental health outcomes. When individuals regularly practice gratitude, they experience reduced stress, anxiety, and depression. This enhanced mental well-being enables them to stay focused, make better decisions, and persevere through challenges, ultimately contributing to success.

3. Enhanced Relationships

Gratitude fosters stronger social connections. When individuals express gratitude to others, it strengthens their relationships and builds trust. These positive connections often lead to collaboration, support, and opportunities for success.

EXAMPLE

Once upon a time, in the bustling city of Mumbai, India, during the challenging days of the COVID-19 pandemic, a heartwarming story unfolded that showcased the incredible power of gratitude and its profound impact on success.

Dr Naina Kapoor, a dedicated and tireless doctor, was at the forefront of Mumbai's battle against the deadly virus. Alongside her, a remarkable team of paramedical professionals and police personnel worked relentlessly to safeguard their city's residents. Their sacrifices were inspiring, but the weight of their responsibilities was immense.

One evening, as Dr. Kapoor and her team were finishing another exhausting day at the crowded COVID ward, she decided to share a heartfelt message of gratitude. She gathered her colleagues and began:

"Team, I know these times are incredibly challenging. Our days are long, and the circumstances are tougher than we ever imagined. But today, I want to remind you of something powerful - gratitude."

Practicing Gratitude Daily

1. Gratitude Journaling

One of the most popular ways to practice gratitude is through journaling. Each day, write down three to five things you are grateful for. This simple practice helps you focus on the positive aspects of your life and encourages you to seek out moments of gratitude.

2. Expressing Gratitude to Others

Take the time to express your gratitude to people in your life. Whether through spoken or written words, expressing appreciation can strengthen relationships and create a positive environment at work and at home.

3. Mindful Gratitude

Incorporate gratitude into your daily mindfulness practice. During moments of mindfulness or meditation, focus on the things you are grateful for. This reinforces a sense of appreciation and positivity.

4. Reflecting on the Day

Before going to bed, reflect on your day and identify moments of gratitude. Consider the positive experiences, interactions, and accomplishments. This practice can help you go to sleep with a more positive and grateful mindset.

EXAMPLE

Dr Kapoor went on to explain how the practice of gratitude had transformed her own life during the pandemic. She shared how each day, before heading to the hospital, she would reflect on the things she was grateful for. It was a simple practice, yet it changed her perspective entirely.

"Gratitude doesn't just make us feel better," she explained, "It also has a direct link to our success. When we focus on what we have, it fuels our determination, resilience, and compassion."

Her words resonated deeply with her team, and they decided to adopt the practice together. Each day, before starting their shifts, they would take a moment to share something they were grateful for, whether it was the support of their families, the strength of their colleagues, or the smiles of recovered patients.

Shifting Perspective

1. Gratitude for Challenges

Shift your perspective by finding gratitude, even in challenging situations. Instead of dwelling on the difficulty of a problem, consider what you can learn from it and how it can contribute to your growth and development.

2. Gratitude for Small Things

Practice gratitude for the small, everyday things that are easy to overlook, such as a warm cup of coffee, a beautiful sunset, or a kind word from a colleague. Recognising these small moments of joy can increase your overall sense of gratitude.

3. Mindful Presence

Being present in the moment is another way to cultivate gratitude. By fully immersing yourself in the present, you can appreciate the beauty and wonder of life as it unfolds.

EXAMPLE

Over time, the impact of this daily gratitude practice became evident. Dr. Kapoor and her team found themselves approaching their work with renewed energy and a more positive outlook. They were better equipped to deal with the immense stress and emotional toll of the pandemic.

One evening, as Dr. Kapoor and her team were attending to a particularly critical patient, they received a surprise visit from a group of police personnel. These officers had been patrolling the city, ensuring that lockdown measures were followed, and that essential services, like the hospital, could operate safely.

One of the officers, Inspector Rajesh Sharma, spoke on behalf of his team. "We wanted to express our gratitude for your incredible dedication. You are the real heroes of this city, and we are here to support you in any way we can."

Tears welled up in the eyes of the medical team. They were deeply moved by this unexpected show of gratitude from their fellow frontline workers.

Conclusion

Cultivating gratitude is a powerful practice that can transform your life and contribute to your success and well-being. By recognising the positive aspects of your life, regularly practicing gratitude, and shifting your perspective, you can develop a more grateful mindset that enhances your motivation, resilience, and relationships. Gratitude is not only a path to success, but also a key to a more fulfilling and meaningful life.

In the example above, you must have observed that in the midst of a pandemic that tested the limits of human endurance, the practice of gratitude became a beacon of hope for Dr. Kapoor and her team. It reminded them of the collective strength they possessed, the support they received, and the difference they were making in their city.

Through daily expressions of gratitude, their perspective shifted from one of exhaustion and despair to one of resilience and determination. Their success was not just measured in terms of patient recoveries, but also in the bonds they forged and the positive impact they had on each other's lives.

As they continued their valiant efforts to safeguard humanity during the pandemic, Dr. Kapoor and her team carried with them the understanding that gratitude was not just a sentiment; it was a powerful force that connected their hearts, fuelled their spirits, and contributed to their ultimate success in the face of adversity.

– 11 –

A Positive Work Environment

Introduction

A positive work environment is not merely a pleasant place to spend one's working hours; it is a catalyst for employee well-being, engagement, and organisational success. In this paper, we will explore the various facets of creating and sustaining a positive work environment. We will discuss the importance of fostering positivity, leading with a positive mindset, and the benefits of thriving in a supportive workplace.

Creating a Positive Workplace

1. A Culture of Respect and Inclusion

A positive workplace starts with a culture of respect and inclusion. Employees should feel valued and appreciated for their unique contributions and perspectives. Inclusive practices promote diversity and create an environment where everyone feels they belong.

2. Open and Effective Communication

Open and transparent communication is vital for a positive work environment. Encourage employees to voice their opinions, concerns, and ideas without fear of reprisal. Effective communication fosters trust and ensures that everyone is on the same page.

3. Work-Life Balance

Promote work-life balance to prevent burnout and maintain employee well-being. Encourage flexible schedules, remote work options, and opportunities for employees to recharge and take care of their physical and mental health.

4. Recognition and Appreciation

Regularly recognise and appreciate employees for their efforts and achievements. A simple "thank you" or acknowledgement of a job well done can go a long way in boosting morale and motivation.

EXAMPLE

In the heart of New Delhi, there existed a remarkable architectural firm named "Architects of Unity," renowned for its innovative designs and groundbreaking projects. However, what truly set this firm apart was its unwavering commitment to creating a positive work environment, where employees could flourish and contribute to their fullest potential.

The journey to foster a positive work environment at Architects of Unity began with its visionary founder and CEO, Aanya Kapoor. Aanya firmly believed that success was not just about profits, but also about creating a place where every employee felt valued, heard, and motivated.

Step 1: Open Communication

Aanya initiated open communication channels. She held regular team meetings and one-on-one sessions with her employees, encouraging them to voice their opinions, concerns, and ideas freely. Through this transparent approach, employees felt that their voices mattered.

Step 2: Celebrating Diversity

The firm celebrated diversity as a source of strength. Employees from different cultural backgrounds brought unique perspectives to projects. Aanya made sure that diversity and inclusion were not just buzzwords, but lived values within the organisation.

Step 3: The Gratitude Wall

One of the cherished practices at Architects of Unity was the "Gratitude Wall." In the office's common area, employees could pin notes of appreciation and thanks to their colleagues. This simple practice nurtured a culture of appreciation and camaraderie.

Leading with Positivity

1. Leading by Example

Leaders play a pivotal role in creating a positive work environment. When leaders model positive behaviour, attitudes, and emotional intelligence, they set the tone for the entire organisation. Positivity should start at the top and permeate throughout the ranks.

2. Embracing a Growth Mindset

Leaders should foster a growth mindset, emphasising that challenges are opportunities for learning and growth. Encourage employees to view setbacks as stepping stones to success and provide support for their development.

3. Empowering and Supporting Employees

Empower employees to take ownership of their work and provide them with the necessary resources and support. Trust employees to make decisions and contribute to the organisation's success.

4. Constructive Feedback and Coaching

Offer constructive feedback and coaching to help employees grow and improve. Focus on strengths and provide guidance for areas that need development. Encourage a culture of continuous learning and improvement.

EXAMPLE

Aanya Kapoor was not just a CEO; she was a leader who led by example with unwavering positivity. Her leadership style was built on empathy, encouragement, and a deep belief in her team's potential.

Step 4: Leading by Example

Aanya's positivity was contagious. When the firm faced a challenging project that seemed almost impossible to complete on time, Aanya gathered her team. She said, "I have complete faith in each one of you. Together, we can overcome any obstacle with a positive attitude and creative problem-solving."

Step 5: Nurturing Personal Growth

Aanya believed that personal growth was essential for professional success. She encouraged her employees to take up workshops, courses, and certifications. The firm even provided a "Learning Fund" to support employees' continuous learning journeys.

Thriving in a Supportive Environment

1. Enhanced Well-being

A positive work environment contributes to enhanced employee well-being. When employees feel supported, respected, and valued, they are more likely to experience lower stress levels, better mental health, and a higher overall quality of life.

2. Increased Engagement and Productivity

Employees who thrive in a supportive work environment are more engaged and productive. They are motivated to contribute their best efforts and are more likely to go above and beyond in their roles.

3. Higher Retention Rates

Positive work environments lead to higher retention rates. When employees feel satisfied and valued, they are less likely to seek employment elsewhere. This not only reduces turnover costs, but also ensures that the organisation retains valuable talent.

4. Innovation and Creativity

A positive work environment fosters innovation and creativity. When employees feel safe to express their ideas and take risks, they are more likely to come up with groundbreaking solutions and contribute to the organisation's success.

EXAMPLE

Architects of Unity was more than just a workplace; it was a community where employees thrived personally and professionally. The supportive environment wasn't just beneficial for the employees; it had a direct impact on the firm's success.

Step 6: Recognising and Rewarding Efforts

Employees were consistently recognised and rewarded for their hard work and innovative ideas. Monthly awards ceremonies celebrated achievements, motivating others to strive for excellence.

Step 7: Personal Growth Plans

Each employee had a Personal Growth Plan tailored to their career aspirations and development goals. Regular performance reviews focused on employees' strengths and opportunities, ensuring they were on the right path.

Step 8: Nurturing Talents

When Tina, a young architect, joined Architects of Unity, she was a shy and reserved individual. However, the supportive environment and mentorship she received helped her grow into a confident leader within the firm, leading several high-profile projects.

Conclusion

Creating and maintaining a positive work environment is not a one-time task, but an ongoing commitment. It requires leadership that models positivity, fosters a culture of respect and inclusion, and prioritises the well-being and growth of its employees. A positive work environment is not only essential for individual satisfaction and engagement, but also for the long-term success and sustainability of organisations. By nurturing a positive workplace, leaders can unlock the full potential of their teams and create a harmonious and thriving organisational culture.

In the example above, Architects of Unity stood as a testament to the power of a positive work environment in driving success. Aanya Kapoor's vision and leadership had created a workplace where employees felt valued, empowered, and motivated to contribute their best.

As the firm continued to thrive and take on groundbreaking projects, Aanya's philosophy remained steadfast: "Success isn't just about buildings; it's about building a workplace where individuals can flourish, innovate, and find fulfillment in their journey." Architects of Unity demonstrated that when positivity, transparent communication, and a commitment to personal and professional growth were the cornerstones of a workplace, success wasn't just a destination; it was a continuous, joyful journey shared by all.

– 12 –
Overcoming Negativity Bias

Introduction

Negativity bias is a cognitive phenomenon where individuals tend to pay more attention to, remember, and be influenced by negative information, experiences, or emotions compared to positive ones. While this bias may have evolved as an adaptive survival mechanism, it can often hinder personal well-being and decision-making in modern society. This paper explores the concept of negativity bias, strategies for countering it with positivity, and techniques for maintaining a positive mindset during challenging times.

Understanding Negativity Bias

1. Evolutionary Origins

Negativity bias has evolutionary roots that date back to our ancestors' need for survival. Paying extra attention to potential threats and dangers, such as predators or food scarcity, was advantageous for their survival. Consequently, humans developed a heightened sensitivity to negative stimuli.

2. Psychological Impact

In contemporary life, negativity bias manifests as an inclination to focus on and dwell upon negative experiences, emotions, or information. This cognitive tendency can contribute to heightened stress, anxiety, and a generally pessimistic outlook on life. Furthermore, it can negatively affect interpersonal relationships and decision-making processes.

EXAMPLE: Triumph Over Negativity Bias, The Kargil Victory

In the summer of 1999, the jagged peaks of the Kargil region bore witness to one of the most challenging and heroic chapters in the history of the Indian armed forces. The Kargil War, a grim conflict that unfolded against a backdrop of treacherous terrain and determined enemy forces, serves as an enduring testament to the triumph of positivity, valour, and unwavering courage in the face of overwhelming odds.

At the outset of the Kargil War, India faced a daunting challenge. The enemy had seized control of strategic heights, posing an imminent threat to the nation's security. The situation was dire, and the odds seemed insurmountable. It was a classic scenario where negativity bias, the human tendency to fixate on negative information, could have overwhelmed the morale of the Indian armed forces.

Negativity Bias Unleashed

- Reports of enemy incursions, well-fortified bunkers and casualties flowed relentlessly into military command centres.
- The enormity of the situation could have easily led to despondency and inaction among the troops and their leaders.

Countering Negativity with Positivity

1. Awareness

The first step in overcoming negativity bias is cultivating awareness. Recognise when negativity bias is influencing your thoughts and reactions. Acknowledging this bias is essential for initiating change.

2. Cognitive Reframing

Cognitive reframing involves consciously altering the way you perceive and interpret events or situations. When confronted with a negative experience, make an effort to identify a positive or neutral perspective. This practice helps shift your focus from the negative aspects to more constructive and optimistic viewpoints.

3. Gratitude Practice

Regularly practicing gratitude is a powerful strategy for mitigating negativity bias. Dedicate time to reflect upon and appreciate the positive aspects of your life, which can help balance your perspective and foster a more optimistic outlook.

4. Positive Affirmations

Positive affirmations involve repeating affirmative statements to yourself. These statements can challenge and replace negative self-talk, instilling more constructive, and empowering beliefs.

EXAMPLE

So, to understand better, let's go back to our Kargil War story. The Indian armed forces, under the able leadership of officers like Capt. Vikram Batra, Capt. Anuj Nayyar, and Capt. Manoj Pandey, recognised the insidious nature of negativity bias and were determined to confront it head-on.

Changing the Narrative

- Acknowledging the power of positivity, military leaders like Colonel Yogesh Kumar Joshi and Lieutenant General Mohinder Puri infused hope, courage, and determination into the hearts of their soldiers.
- Stories of extraordinary valour and bravery from the frontlines began circulating, inspiring every soldier to believe in the possibility of victory.

Maintaining Positivity in Tough Times

1. Mindfulness and Meditation

Mindfulness and meditation techniques can help maintain a positive mindset during challenging times. By fostering presence and inner calm, these practices enable you to observe your thoughts and emotions without judgement, ultimately promoting a more positive outlook.

2. Seek Support

Dealing with negativity bias in tough situations can be overwhelming on your own. Seek support from friends, family, or a therapist who can offer emotional support, an external perspective, and coping strategies.

3. Self-Compassion

Practicing self-compassion entails treating yourself with the same kindness and understanding you would extend to a friend in difficult times. Embrace patience and self-forgiveness, recognising that setbacks and difficulties are an inherent part of life.

4. Resilience-Building

Building resilience involves developing the skills and mindset to rebound from adversity. By enhancing resilience, you can navigate tough times, sustaining a positive outlook, maintaining your well-being, and achieving personal growth.

EXAMPLE

So, as the conflict intensified, sustaining positivity became an integral aspect of the Indian forces' strategy. Young officers like Captain Vikram Batra and Lieutenant Manoj Pandey led the way, embodying resilience and unwavering positivity.

Captain Vikram Batra, the Sher Shah of Kargil:

- Captain Vikram Batra's iconic words, "Yeh Dil Maange More!" (This heart desires more), encapsulated his unyielding spirit.
- Despite overwhelming odds, he and his team valiantly captured the strategically vital peak of Point 4875 (now renamed Batra Top), serving as an inspiration to the entire nation.

Lieutenant Manoj Pandey, Hero of Batalik:

- Lieutenant Manoj Pandey's bravery during the Battle of Khalubar became legendary. He famously declared, "If death strikes before I prove my blood, I swear, I'll kill death."

- His relentless positivity and determination propelled his platoon to victory in a battle where the odds were overwhelmingly stacked against them.

Major Anuj Nayyar, Braveheart of Jubar Top:

- Major Anuj Nayyar, with his fearless resolve, successfully recaptured Jubar Top, but made the ultimate sacrifice.
- His unwavering dedication to the mission and the positivity he radiated, even in the face of danger, served as a guiding light for his comrades.

The Triumph of Positivity:

Through unwavering determination and indomitable positivity, the Indian armed forces gradually reversed the tide of the Kargil War. The entire nation rallied behind these heroes, and the world witnessed the indomitable spirit of the Indian forces.

The Ultimate Victory:

- Tololing, Tiger Hill, Drass, Mashkoh Valley, and Kargil itself were wrested from the enemy's grasp.
- The Kargil War not only showcased the valour and gallantry of the Indian armed forces but also their resilience in maintaining positivity during one of the most challenging episodes in the nation's history.

Conclusion

Negativity bias is a natural cognitive tendency, but it doesn't have to dominate our thoughts and experiences. By understanding its evolutionary origins, fostering awareness, and implementing strategies for countering negativity with positivity, individuals can overcome this bias and enhance their overall well-being. Additionally, maintaining a positive mindset during challenging times through mindfulness, seeking support, practicing self-compassion, and building resilience empowers individuals to navigate adversity while preserving their optimism and achieving personal growth. Ultimately, the ability to overcome negativity bias and cultivate positivity lies within our reach, promoting a more balanced and fulfilling life.

The Kargil War stands as a poignant testament to humanity's capacity to overcome negativity bias with unwavering positivity. Young officers like Captain Vikram Batra, Lieutenant Manoj Pandey, and Major Anuj Nayyar, along with the countless soldiers who fought alongside them, embodied the spirit of resilience and hope.

In the face of extreme adversity, they recognised the power of positivity and actively countered negativity bias. Through their indomitable will, they transformed despair into hope and uncertainty into victory. The Kargil War remains an eternal source of inspiration, reminding us all that positivity, even in the direst of circumstances, can lead to triumph and success.

– 13 –

Celebrating Success

Introduction

Celebrating success is a crucial aspect of personal and professional growth. It involves recognising achievements, acknowledging the effort and dedication that went into them, and reaping the positive benefits that come with celebration. In this paper, we will explore the significance of celebrating success, its impact on reinforcing positive habits, and the role it plays in motivation and well-being.

Recognising Achievements

1. Acknowledging Milestones

Celebrating success begins with acknowledging milestones and achievements, both big and small. Whether it's completing a project at work, reaching a fitness goal, or achieving a personal milestone, recognising these accomplishments is the first step in the celebration process.

2. Embracing a Growth Mindset

Acknowledging achievements encourages the development of a growth mindset. When individuals recognise their progress and accomplishments, they are more likely to believe in their ability to learn, grow, and achieve even more in the future.

EXAMPLE: The Victory of the Human Spirit

In the world of sports, there is a universal truth: celebrating success isn't just about the final score; it's about the journey, the unwavering determination, and the unbreakable spirit that drive athletes to extraordinary achievements. Let's explore the importance of recognising achievements, the significance of celebration, and how it reinforces positive habits through the story of an underdog who defied all odds.

Let's understand the concept better from a story...

In the small town of Ganga Nagar, India, there lived a young boy named Arjun. Arjun was an ordinary lad with an extraordinary passion for athletics. He had a natural flair for sprinting, and his dream was to represent his country on the global stage.

Step 1: Arjun's Dedication

From a young age, Arjun displayed a level of dedication that was unmatched. He tirelessly trained, pushing himself to the limits and setting personal records that were nothing short of remarkable.

Step 2: Coach's Recognition

Arjun's coach, Mr. Kapoor, recognised his prodigious talent and unwavering commitment. He encouraged Arjun to compete in local and regional races, where he consistently outshone his competitors.

Step 3: Arjun's Rising Star

As Arjun's victories piled up, he started gaining attention not just locally, but also nationally. His achievements were celebrated in his town, and he began to receive invitations to compete at the state level.

The Importance of Celebration

1. Boosting Motivation

Celebrating success serves as a powerful motivator. When individuals see the fruits of their labour celebrated and rewarded, it encourages them to continue working towards their goals. The prospect of future celebrations becomes a driving force for ongoing success.

2. Enhancing Well-being

Celebration contributes to overall well-being by promoting a positive mindset and reducing stress. The act of celebrating success releases endorphins, which are known as "feel-good" hormones, creating a sense of happiness and contentment.

3. Strengthening Relationships

Celebrating success can strengthen interpersonal relationships. When individuals share their accomplishments with friends, family, or colleagues, it fosters a sense of connection and social support. Celebrating together can deepen bonds and create a supportive network.

EXAMPLE

Arjun's journey was marked not just by personal victories, but also by the celebrations that followed each success.

Step 4: Motivating Arjun

Celebrations after each win motivated Arjun to strive for more. The applause, medals, and cheers of his family and friends were a constant reminder of his potential.

Step 5: Forging Bonds

Celebrating success helped Arjun forge deep bonds with his fellow athletes and competitors. Rivalries turned into friendships as they acknowledged each other's achievements.

Step 6: The Town's Pride

Arjun's success became a source of pride for Ganga Nagar. His achievements were celebrated as a reflection of the town's spirit and resilience.

Reinforcing Positive Habits

1. Habit Formation

Celebrating success plays a pivotal role in habit formation. When individuals celebrate the positive habits and behaviours that led to their achievements, they reinforce those habits. This makes it more likely that these behaviours will become ingrained in their daily lives.

2. Positive Reinforcement

Positive reinforcement through celebration reinforces the idea that effort and hard work lead to positive outcomes. It encourages individuals to continue practicing the behaviours and habits that contributed to their success.

3. Sustaining Momentum

Celebration helps individuals maintain momentum in their pursuits. After achieving one goal, celebrating it provides the motivation and energy to set new goals and continue making progress.

EXAMPLE

Arjun's relentless pursuit of excellence and his celebration of achievements reinforced positive habits that set him apart from the competition.

Step 7: Learning from Losses

Arjun didn't just celebrate victories; he also embraced his losses as opportunities to learn and grow. Each setback only fuelled his determination to succeed.

Step 8: Healthy Competition

Celebrating success encouraged healthy competition. Arjun's competitors were inspired by his victories and pushed themselves to perform at their best.

Step 9: Inspiring the Next Generation

Arjun's journey and celebrations inspired the younger generation of athletes in Ganga Nagar. They looked up to him as a role model and aspired to follow in his footsteps.

The Ultimate Victory

Arjun's journey, marked by his dedication, celebrations, and positive habits, led him to the pinnacle of his sport. He not only represented his country but also won a gold medal in a prestigious international competition.

Conclusion

Celebrating success is an integral part of personal and professional growth. By recognising achievements, understanding the importance of celebration, and acknowledging its role in reinforcing positive habits, individuals can enhance their motivation, well-being, and overall quality of life. Celebrating success not only provides a sense of accomplishment but also serves as a reminder that hard work and dedication are rewarded. As individuals continue to acknowledge their achievements and celebrate their successes, they create a positive cycle of growth and development that propels them towards even greater accomplishments in the future.

Arjun's story is a testament to the power of celebrating success in the world of sports. It underscores the importance of recognising achievements, the significance of celebration, and how it reinforces positive habits in athletes. Beyond the medals and records, it's the journey, the bonds formed, and the joy of celebrating every hard-fought victory that truly defines success in sports. Arjun's story is a reminder that in the arena of life, the spirit of celebration is a powerful ally on the path to achieving greatness.

– 14 –

Beyond Success:
A Fulfilling Life

Introduction

While achieving success is a common pursuit in life, it is essential to recognise that success alone does not necessarily equate to a fulfilling life. True fulfilment often goes beyond success and encompasses aspects such as well-being, contributing to others, and finding meaning and purpose. In this chapter, we will explore these dimensions of a fulfilling life and how they can complement traditional notions of success.

Balancing Success and Well-being

In our quest for success, we often find ourselves on a relentless treadmill of achievement, chasing goals and milestones. While success is a significant aspect of our lives, it's essential to recognise that true fulfilment goes beyond the mere accumulation of accomplishments. In this chapter, we'll explore the practical aspects of leading a fulfilling life by balancing success and well-being, contributing to others, and finding meaning and purpose in our everyday existence.

1. The Pursuit of Well-being

Well-being is a holistic concept that encompasses physical, mental, and emotional health, as well as overall life satisfaction. When pursuing success, it's crucial to prioritise well-being. Neglecting well-being can lead to burnout, stress, and a diminished sense of fulfilment.

2. Finding Balance

Balancing success and well-being involves setting boundaries, managing stress, and incorporating self-care practices into your daily routine. By doing so, individuals can maintain their health and energy levels, ensuring they have the vitality to enjoy the fruits of their success.

3. Reevaluating Success

Consider reevaluating your definition of success to include well-being as a fundamental component. A fulfilling life integrates achievements with a sense of contentment, happiness, and overall well-being.

Day-to-Day Example: The Work-Life Balancer

Meet Maya, a marketing executive who was once consumed by her work. She would regularly clock long hours at the office, consistently chasing promotions and pay raises. Her success was undeniable, but her well-being suffered.

Maya decided to make a change

Step 1: Prioritising Well-being

Maya began by allocating time each day for self-care. She embraced morning meditation, regular exercise, and a balanced diet to nurture her physical and mental health.

Step 2: Setting Boundaries

She realised the importance of setting boundaries at work. Maya started leaving the office on time and encouraged her team to do the same. She discovered that quality work could be accomplished without compromising her well-being.

Step 3: Celebrating Small Wins

Maya learned to celebrate small achievements in her personal life, such as completing a challenging workout or spending quality time with loved ones. These celebrations added a sense of fulfillment to her daily routine.

Contributing to Others

1. The Power of Contribution

Contributing to others is a significant source of fulfilment. Acts of kindness, generosity, and service to others not only benefit the recipients, but also bring a sense of purpose and joy to the giver.

2. Building Meaningful Relationships

Positive relationships and connections with others are central to a fulfilling life. Building meaningful relationships through empathy, compassion, and support not only enhances one's sense of purpose, but also enriches life experiences.

3. Volunteering and Philanthropy

Engaging in volunteering or philanthropic activities provides opportunities to make a positive impact on the community and the world. These acts of service can be deeply fulfilling, allowing individuals to contribute to causes they are passionate about.

Day-to-Day Example: The Neighbourhood Helper

Imagine Raj, a software engineer, who decided to channel his skills for a greater purpose. He began volunteering to teach coding to underprivileged children in his neighbourhood.

Step 1: Identifying a Cause

Raj identified a cause that resonated with him: empowering young minds through education. He realised that contributing to the community gave his life a deeper sense of fulfilment.

Step 2: Regular Commitment

Raj dedicated a few hours each week to teaching coding to local children. He found joy in witnessing their progress and growth.

Step 3: Expanding Impact

Over time, Raj's passion led him to inspire other neighbours to join his cause. Together, they created a supportive community dedicated to enhancing the lives of these children.

Finding Meaning and Purpose

1. The Search for Meaning

Finding meaning and purpose is a fundamental human need. A fulfilling life often involves aligning one's actions and goals with a sense of purpose that goes beyond personal gain.

2. Self-Reflection

Take time for self-reflection to explore your values, passions, and what truly matters to you. This process can help uncover your unique purpose and guide your life choices.

3. Pursuing Passion Projects

Pursuing passion projects or hobbies that align with your values and interests can provide a sense of meaning and purpose. These activities allow you to express your creativity and contribute to your personal growth.

Day-to-Day Example: The Life Explorer

Meet Aisha, an accountant who felt stuck in her routine. She yearned for a more profound meaning in her life.

Step 1: Self-Reflection

Aisha embarked on a journey of self-discovery. She reflected on her passions, values, and what truly mattered to her.

Step 2: Pursuing Passions

She began integrating her passions into her daily life. Aisha explored hobbies like painting and writing, which brought her immense joy.

Step 3: Living with Purpose

As Aisha continued her exploration, she realised that her purpose extended beyond her job. She started volunteering at an animal shelter, combining her love for animals with her newfound sense of purpose.

Conclusion

Leading a fulfilling life doesn't require grand gestures or radical transformations. It's often about making conscious choices in our day-to-day existence. By balancing success and well-being, contributing to others, and finding meaning and purpose in our everyday actions, we can craft a life that transcends the limitations of conventional success.

Through practical steps like prioritising well-being, setting boundaries, and celebrating small achievements, we can enhance our daily lives. By engaging in acts of kindness, supporting our communities, and spreading positivity, we contribute to the well-being of others. And, by seeking self-discovery, pursuing passions, and aligning our actions with our values, we find the profound meaning and purpose that make life truly fulfilling.

Incorporating these principles into our daily routines empowers us to lead lives rich in both success and fulfilment, where each day becomes an opportunity to create a meaningful and purpose-driven existence.

A fulfilling life goes beyond the traditional markers of success and involves a balanced pursuit of well-being, contribution to others, and finding meaning and purpose. Balancing success with well-being ensures that achievement is not at the expense of health and happiness. Contributing to others enhances connections and brings a sense of purpose. Finding meaning and purpose in life provides a deeper sense of fulfilment that transcends external accomplishments.

Ultimately, a fulfilling life is a journey that requires self-awareness, introspection, and a commitment to nurturing well-being, fostering positive relationships, and aligning your actions with your values and passions. By integrating these dimensions into your life, you can lead a life that is not only successful, but also deeply satisfying and meaningful.

Conclusion: A Lifetime of Success Through Positivity

As we draw the curtains on this inspiring journey through the realms of positivity and success, we find ourselves standing at the intersection of dreams and reality. This book has taken us on an exploration of the incredible influence of positivity on the various facets of life, from personal triumphs to building thriving communities, all through the lens of real-world examples from India.

Let's revisit a few of these awe-inspiring Indian narratives that underscore the transformative potential of positivity:

1. Dr. APJ Abdul Kalam: Known as the "People's President," Dr. Kalam's remarkable journey from a small town in Tamil Nadu to the highest office in the land exemplifies the profound impact of a positive mindset. His unwavering belief in the power of education and his commitment to youth empowerment continue to inspire generations.

2. Sudha Murthy: The chairperson of Infosys Foundation, Sudha Murthy's life is a testament

to the incredible outcomes that can be achieved when success is rooted in compassion and philanthropy. Her tireless efforts to improve the lives of countless underprivileged individuals embody the positive change that one person can bring about.

3. Milkha Singh: Fondly known as the "Flying Sikh," Milkha Singh's journey from the blood-soaked fields of Partition to becoming one of India's most celebrated athletes is a story of resilience, determination, and unyielding positivity. His commitment to hard work and unwavering focus on his goals continues to inspire athletes across the nation.

4. Kiran Mazumdar-Shaw: As the founder of Biocon, Kiran Mazumdar-Shaw's pioneering spirit in the field of biotechnology has not only revolutionised healthcare but also shattered gender stereotypes in the business world. Her journey serves as a beacon of hope for aspiring entrepreneurs who dare to dream.

These luminous figures from India stand as living proof that positivity is the cornerstone of personal and societal transformation. But how can you, our reader, embark on a similar journey of positivity and lifelong success? Here are hints and broader outlines to guide you:

Appendix A: Exercises and Activities for Developing a Positive Attitude

This section is a treasure trove of actionable exercises and activities meticulously designed to nurture a positive attitude. From daily gratitude practices and visualisation techniques, to mindfulness routines and self-affirmations, these exercises will empower you to cultivate positivity as a habitual part of your life.

Incorporating positivity into your daily life is a transformative journey that requires practice and dedication. These exercises and activities are meticulously designed to help you cultivate a positive attitude and make positivity a habit.

1. Daily Gratitude Journal

Objective: To foster gratitude and shift your focus towards positive aspects of your life.

How to Do It:

1. Set aside a few minutes each day, preferably in the morning or before bedtime.
2. Write down three to five things you're grateful for. They can be big or small, from your health and loved ones, to a delicious meal, or a beautiful sunrise.
3. Reflect on why you're grateful for each item on your list.
4. Over time, this practice will train your mind to seek and appreciate the positive aspects of your life.

2. Positive Affirmations

Objective: To boost self-esteem, confidence, and a positive self-image.

How to Do It:

1. Create a list of positive affirmations that resonate with you. Examples include "I am capable," "I am worthy of love and success," or "I embrace challenges as opportunities."
2. Stand in front of a mirror, look into your own eyes and repeat these affirmations aloud. Do this daily, ideally in the morning.
3. Visualise each affirmation as you say it. Imagine yourself embodying the qualities and beliefs expressed in the affirmations.

4. Over time, these positive self-messages will influence your thoughts and behaviours, leading to increased positivity.

3. Mindfulness Meditation

Objective: To cultivate awareness, reduce stress, and stay present in the moment.

How to Do It:

1. Find a quiet, comfortable place to sit or lie down.
2. Close your eyes and take a few deep breaths to centre yourself.
3. Focus your attention on your breath. Pay close attention to the sensation of each inhale and exhale.
4. As thoughts enter your mind, acknowledge them without judgement, and gently redirect your focus to your breath.
5. Start with short sessions (5-10 minutes), and gradually increase the duration as you become more comfortable.
6. Practicing mindfulness daily helps you build resilience and a positive outlook on life.

4. Acts of Kindness

Objective: To experience the joy of giving and increase feelings of positivity.

How to Do It:

1. Make a list of small acts of kindness you can perform daily or weekly, such as sending a thoughtful message, helping a neighbour, or donating to a charity.
2. Commit to doing at least one act of kindness each day.
3. Notice the positive emotions and sense of fulfilment that arise from these actions.
4. As you continue, you'll find that kindness not only brightens others' lives, but also enhances your own positivity.

5. Visualisation and Goal-Setting

Objective: To harness the power of positive visualisation to achieve your goals.

How to Do It:

1. Sit in a quiet, comfortable space.
2. Close your eyes and take a few deep breaths to relax.
3. Visualise your goals as if you've already achieved them. Imagine the sights, sounds, and emotions associated with your success.
4. Create a detailed mental image of your desired outcome.
5. Practice this visualisation daily, allowing it to fuel your motivation and belief in your ability to succeed.

6. Morning Positivity Routine

Objective: To start your day with a positive mindset.

How to Do It:

1. Create a morning routine that includes activities like gratitude journaling, positive affirmations, and visualisation.
2. Dedicate 10-15 minutes each morning to these activities before you begin your day.
3. This routine will set a positive tone for your day and help you approach challenges with a more optimistic outlook.

7. Positive Visualisation Board

Objective: To create a visual representation of your goals and aspirations.

How to Do It:

1. Collect images, quotes, and symbols that represent your goals, dreams, and positive affirmations.
2. Create a physical or digital vision board using these elements.
3. Place your vision board where you can see it daily, such as on your bedroom wall or as your computer wallpaper.
4. Regularly engage with your vision board to reinforce your positive mindset and remind yourself of your aspirations.

8. Reflective Journaling

Objective: To gain insight into your thoughts and emotions, and promote self-awareness.

How to Do It:

1. Dedicate time each day to reflect on your thoughts and experiences.
2. Write about your successes, challenges, and the emotions you've experienced.
3. Identify patterns in your thinking and explore ways to reframe negative thoughts into more positive ones.
4. Journaling helps you become more self-aware and encourages a positive mindset.

9. Nature Connection

Objective: To experience the rejuvenating power of nature.

How to Do It:

1. Spend time in nature, whether it's a walk in the park, a hike in the woods, or simply sitting in your garden.
2. Practice mindfulness by fully engaging your senses in the natural surroundings. Observe the sights, sounds, smells, and textures.

3. Feel a sense of awe and gratitude for the beauty and tranquillity of nature.

4. Regular nature outings can help reduce stress and increase your overall sense of positivity.

10. Positive Reading Material

Objective: To surround yourself with positive influences.

How to Do It:

1. Curate a list of books, articles, and websites that inspire and uplift you.

2. Allocate time each day or week for reading or listening to positive content.

3. Engaging with positive material can reinforce your optimistic mindset and provide ongoing motivation.

Remember that cultivating a positive attitude is an ongoing process. Consistency is key. Incorporate these exercises and activities into your daily or weekly routine, and, over time, you'll find yourself naturally embracing a more positive outlook on life.

In conclusion, always remember that success is not confined to external achievements, but extends to the profound sense of fulfilment, positivity, and purpose that permeates every facet of your life. As you embark on this lifelong odyssey, grasp that positivity is not just a final destination, but the very path leading to a lifetime of success, personal growth, and enduring happiness. Embrace it, nurture it, and watch in awe as it transforms your life in ways you could never have imagined.

of success, personal growth, and enduring happiness. Embrace it, nurture it, and watch in awe as it transforms your life in ways you could never have imagined.

Acknowledgement

We are profoundly grateful to everyone who contributed to the creation of this book on attitude. This journey has been a collective effort, and we couldn't have accomplished it without the amazing support and encouragement we received.

First, we want to express our heartfelt thanks to our families and friends for their steadfast support, patience, and belief in us. Your encouragement kept us motivated through every obstacle, reminding us of the significance of the attitudes we discuss.

We also extend our deep appreciation to our colleagues , whose valuable insights and constructive feedback helped shape our ideas into the book you hold in your hands. Your guidance has been essential.

Our sincere gratitude goes to Notion Press for believing in our vision and providing us with a platform to share our thoughts on attitude. Your commitment to this project has been truly remarkable.

Lastly, we want to acknowledge each other for the mutual respect, collaboration, and shared dedication to this book. Writing together has been a deeply fulfilling experience, and we take pride in the message we've created as a team.

To everyone who inspired, guided, or supported us throughout this journey—thank you. This book reflects all the positive attitudes that have impacted our lives, and we hope it will inspire others as well.

About the Authors

Reshmi Menon: Reshmi Menon is a highly respected and decorated recruiter in the world of campus placements. She currently holds the position of Lead for Early Talent Acquisition in India and the Asia-Pacific region, working for product companies. Menon was recently awarded the recruiter of the Year Award by the Honorable Minister Chamakura Malla Reddy of Labor and Employment in Telangana. Furthermore, the All India Council for Technical Education (AICTE), Government of India, recently felicitated Menon as an Innovative Recruiter, honouring the vision of the Prime Minister to provide 10 million internships by 2025. The former AICTE Chairman, Dr Sahastrabudhey, also recognised Menon for offering the most virtual internships in 2022. Menon's impressive accolades include five best HR awards from Calgary, Canada, in 2009 and 2010 and three more in India. With a graduate degree in management from Bangalore University and an MBA in HR (pursuing) from IIM Kozhikode, Menon brings over 17 years of rich experience in recruitment across India, the US, the Asia-Pacific region, Europe, the Middle East, and Africa.

Drawing from her extensive expertise in campus hiring for international cities and her hands-on experience in recruiting young talent, Menon offers readers valuable insights to maximise their potential through the power of a positive mindset.

Rajat Pathak: Rajat Pathak holds a bachelor's degree in commerce from Calcutta University and a postgraduate degree in marketing and sales management from Bhartiya Vidya Bhawan. He also has a Ph.D. in management. Pathak boasts an extensive and distinguished career in channel sales, with expertise in dealers and distribution networks. He has held positions at prominent organisations such as Castrol India, Jindal Swastik Pipes Limited, and REPSOL YPF, accumulating over 25 years of experience in the manufacturing, automobile, lubricants, service, and higher education industries. Pathak's diverse experience includes strategic planning, brand and product management, corporate governance, people management, academic and non-academic training, business development, brand positioning and enhancement, event and vendor management, team leadership, corporate relations, and network development. He currently serves as the Director of Corporate Relations at Amity University Madhya Pradesh, where he oversees strategic management and academic/training portfolios.